our best BABY AFGHANS

When you — or someone close to you — receive the exciting news that a baby is on the way, turn to this precious collection of afghans for the perfect "birth-day" present. Gathered from favorite Leisure Arts leaflets and magazines, Our Best Baby Afghans contains 54 cover-ups that are as special and unique as baby! You'll find a darling array of throws for little girls, from fanciful wraps with flirty ruffles to classic comforters in pretty pastels. Or you can shower the little princess with a bouquet of floral afghans. There are also lots of playful throws for little boys, from blue and white blankets to afghans with twirling pinwheels and sporty stripes. And there are plenty of patterns that are appropriate for him or her! We used a variety of yarns to create the sweet wraps in this treasury, so you'll always find an afghan suitable for the season. And because these little afghans work up quickly, you'll have time to make one (or more!) for each of the babies in your life!

LEISURE ARTS, INC.
Little Rock, Arkansas

our best BABY AFGHANS

EDITORIAL STAFF

Vice President and Editor-in-Chief:
Anne Van Wagner Childs
Executive Director: Sandra Graham Case
Editorial Director: Susan Frantz Wiles
Publications Director: Carla Bentley
Creative Art Director: Gloria Bearden
Production Art Director: Melinda Stout

EDITORIAL
Managing Editor: Linda L. Trimble
Senior Associate Editor: Darla Burdette Kelsay
Associate Editor: Robyn Sheffield-Edwards
Assistant Editors: Tammi Williamson Bradley and
Terri Leming Davidson
Copy Editor: Laura Lee Weland

PRODUCTION
Managing Editor: Susan White Sullivan
Senior Technical Editor: Cathy Hardy
Senior Instructional Editor: Joan Beebe
Instructional Editors: Susan Ackerman,
Sherry L. Berry, Sue Galucki, Sarah J. Green,
Carol Hall, Valesha Marshell Kirksey, Frances
Moore-Kyle, Jeanne A. Lowes, Katherine
Satterfield Robert, and Jackie Botnik Stanfill

ART
Book Art Director: Rhonda Hodge Shelby
Senior Production Artist: Sonya McFatrich
Production Artists: Roberta Aulwes, Katie Murphy,
Dana Vaughn, and Katherine Yancey
Photography Stylists: Sondra Daniel, Karen Hall,
Aurora Huston, Christina Tiano Myers, and
Zaneta Senger

BUSINESS STAFF

Publisher: Bruce Akin
Vice President, Finance: Tom Siebenmorgen
Vice President, Retail Sales: Thomas L. Carlisle
Retail Sales Director: Richard Tignor
Vice President, Retail Marketing: Pam Stebbins
Retail Marketing Director: Margaret Sweetin
Retail Customer Services Manager: Carolyn Pruss

General Merchandise Manager: Russ Barnett
Distribution Director: Ed M. Strackbein
Vice President, Marketing: Guy A. Crossley
Marketing Manager: Byron L. Taylor
Print Production Manager: Laura Lockhart
Print Production Coordinator: Nancy Reddick Baker

Library of Congress Catalog Number: 96-76049
International Standard Book Number 1-57486-042-9

table of contents

enchanting diamonds

This beautiful keepsake afghan will enchant Mother and baby.
Fashioned in white worsted weight yarn, the lacy throw features an
openwork pattern of diamonds and has an exquisite edging.

Finished Size: Approximately 38" x 48"

MATERIALS
   Worsted Weight Yarn, approximately:
      25 ounces, (710 grams, 1,460 yards)
   Crochet hook, size G (4.00 mm) **or** size needed
      for gauge

GAUGE: In pattern, 2 repeats and 13 rows = 3½"

Gauge Swatch: (5½" x 3½")
Ch 26 **loosely**.
Work same as Center for 13 rows.
Finish off.

CENTER
Ch 130 **loosely**.
Row 1 (Right side)**:** Sc in second ch from hook and in
next 2 chs, ch 5, ★ skip next 3 chs, sc in next 5 chs,
ch 5; repeat from ★ across to last 6 chs, skip next
3 chs, sc in last 3 chs: 81 sc.
Note: Loop a short piece of yarn around any stitch to
mark last row as **right** side.
Row 2: Ch 1, turn; sc in first 2 sc, ch 3, sc in next
loop, ch 3, ★ skip next sc, sc in next 3 sc, ch 3, sc in
next loop, ch 3; repeat from ★ across to last 3 sc, skip
next sc, sc in last 2 sc: 65 sc.
Row 3: Ch 1, turn; sc in first sc, ★ ch 3, sc in next
ch-3 sp, sc in next sc and in next ch-3 sp, ch 3, skip
next sc, sc in next sc; repeat from ★ across.
Row 4: Ch 5 **(counts as first dc plus ch 2, now
and throughout)**, turn; sc in first ch-3 sp, sc in next
3 sc and in next ch-3 sp, ★ ch 5, sc in next ch-3 sp,
sc in next 3 sc and in next ch-3 sp; repeat from ★
across to last sc, ch 2, dc in last sc: 80 sc.
Row 5: Ch 1, turn; sc in first dc, ch 3, skip next sc,
sc in next 3 sc, ch 3, ★ sc in next loop, ch 3, skip
next sc, sc in next 3 sc, ch 3; repeat from ★ across to
last dc, sc in last dc: 65 sc.

Row 6: Ch 1, turn; sc in first sc and in next ch-3 sp,
ch 3, skip next sc, sc in next sc, ch 3, ★ sc in next
ch-3 sp, sc in next sc and in next ch-3 sp, ch 3, skip
next sc, sc in next sc, ch 3; repeat from ★ across to
last ch-3 sp, sc in last ch-3 sp and in last sc.
Row 7: Ch 1, turn; sc in first 2 sc and in next ch-3
sp, ch 5, ★ sc in next ch-3 sp, sc in next 3 sc and in
next ch-3 sp, ch 5; repeat from ★ across to last ch-3
sp, sc in last ch-3 sp and in last 2 sc: 81 sc.
Repeat Rows 2-7 until Center measures approximately
38" from beginning ch, ending by working Row 7.
Do **not** finish off.

EDGING
Rnd 1: Ch 1, do **not** turn; work 181 sc evenly
spaced across end of rows; working in free loops of
beginning ch *(Fig. 23b, page 125)*, 3 sc in first ch,
work 133 sc evenly spaced across to last ch, 3 sc in
last ch; work 181 sc evenly spaced across end of rows;
working in Back Loops Only of last row *(Fig. 22,
page 125)*, 3 sc in first sc, work 133 sc evenly spaced
across to last sc, 3 sc in last sc; join with slip st to first
sc: 640 sc.
Rnd 2: Working in both loops, slip st in next 4 sc,
ch 1, sc in same st and in next 4 sc, ch 5, skip next
3 sc, ★ sc in next 5 sc, ch 5, skip next 3 sts; repeat
from ★ around; join with slip st to first sc: 400 sc.
Rnd 3: Slip st in next sc, ch 1, sc in same st and in
next 2 sc, ch 3, sc in next loop, ch 3, ★ skip next sc,
sc in next 3 sc, ch 3, sc in next loop, ch 3; repeat
from ★ around; join with slip st to first sc: 320 sc.
Rnd 4: Slip st in next sc, ch 1, sc in same st, ch 5, sc
in next ch-3 sp, sc in next sc and in next ch-3 sp,
ch 5, ★ skip next sc, sc in next sc, ch 5, sc in next
ch-3 sp, sc in next sc and in next ch-3 sp, ch 5; repeat
from ★ around; join with slip st to first sc.
Rnd 5: Slip st in next 4 chs, ch 1, sc in same loop,
sc in next 3 sc and in next loop, ch 5, ★ sc in next
loop, sc in next 3 sc and in next loop, ch 5; repeat
from ★ around; join with slip st to first sc: 400 sc.

Rnds 6 and 7: Repeat Rnds 3 and 4.

Rnd 8: Slip st in next 4 chs, ch 1, sc in same loop, sc in next 3 sc and in next loop, ch 7, ★ sc in next loop, sc in next 3 sc and in next loop, ch 7; repeat from ★ around; join with slip st to first sc: 400 sc.

Rnd 9: Slip st in next sc, ch 1, sc in same st and in next 2 sc, ch 5, sc in next loop, ch 5, ★ skip next sc, sc in next 3 sc, ch 5, sc in next loop, ch 5; repeat from ★ around; join with slip st to first sc: 320 sc.

Rnd 10: Slip st in next sc, ch 1, sc in same st, ch 7, sc in next loop, sc in next sc and in next loop, ch 7, ★ skip next sc, sc in next sc, ch 7, sc in next loop, sc in next sc and in next loop, ch 7; repeat from ★ around; join with slip st to first sc.

Rnd 11: Slip st in next 6 chs, ch 1, sc in same loop, sc in next 3 sc and in next loop, ch 7, ★ sc in next loop, sc in next 3 sc and in next loop, ch 7; repeat from ★ around; join with slip st to first sc: 400 sc.

Rnd 12: Slip st in next sc, ch 1, sc in same st and in next 2 sc, ch 7, sc in next loop, ch 7, ★ skip next sc, sc in next 3 sc, ch 7, sc in next loop, ch 7; repeat from ★ around; join with slip st to first sc: 320 sc.

Rnd 13: Slip st in next sc, ch 1, sc in same st, ch 7, sc in next loop and in next sc, ch 6, slip st in top of sc just made, sc in next loop, ch 7, ★ skip next sc, sc in next sc, ch 7, sc in next loop and in next sc, ch 6, slip st in top of sc just made, sc in next loop, ch 7; repeat from ★ around; join with slip st to first sc, finish off.

*Worked in strips of motifs that are joined as you go,
this adorable afghan is abloom with pretty posies.
A picot edging completes the dainty blanket.*

Finished Size: Approximately 37" x 45"

MATERIALS
Sport Weight Yarn, approximately:
Color A (White) - 4½ ounces,
(130 grams, 425 yards)
Color B (Green) - 4½ ounces,
(130 grams, 425 yards)
Color C (Pink) - 4½ ounces,
(130 grams, 425 yards)
Crochet hook, size G (4.00 mm) **or** size needed
for gauge

GAUGE: Strip of 3 Motifs = 1½" x 5¼"
Strip = 3½" x 44"

PATTERN STITCHES
SHELL
(Dc, ch 1, dc, ch 2, dc, ch 1, dc) in ch-3 sp
indicated.
DECREASE
★ YO, insert hook in **next** ch-1 sp (at joining), YO
and pull up a loop, YO and draw through 2 loops
on hook; repeat from ★ once **more**, YO and draw
through all 3 loops on hook.
PICOT
Ch 3, hdc in third ch from hook.

FIRST STRIP
FIRST MOTIF
Rnd 1 (Right side)**:** With Color C, ch 4, 2 dc in
fourth ch from hook, ch 3, (3 dc in same st, ch 3) 3
times; join with slip st to top of beginning ch, finish
off: 4 ch-3 sps.

SECOND MOTIF
Rnd 1: With Color C, ch 4, 2 dc in fourth ch from
hook, (ch 3, 3 dc in same st) 3 times, ch 1, drop loop
from hook; with **right** side of **previous Motif** facing,
insert hook in second ch of any ch-3, hook dropped
loop and draw through, ch 1; join with slip st to top of
beginning ch on **new Motif**, finish off.

Repeat Second Motif 22 times **more**, joining **new
Motifs** to ch-3 opposite **previous** joining: 24 Motifs.

EDGING
Rnd 1: With **right** side facing, join Color B with slip
st in ch-3 sp at end of Strip; ch 4, (dc, ch 2, dc, ch 1,
dc) in same sp, ch 1, (work Shell in next ch-3 sp,
ch 1, decrease, ch 1) 23 times, (work Shell in next
ch-3 sp, ch 1) 3 times, (decrease, ch 1, work Shell in
next ch-3 sp, ch 1) across; join with slip st to third ch
of beginning ch-4, finish off: 50 Shells.
Rnd 2: With **right** side facing, join Color A with sc
in sp before Shell at end of Strip *(see Joining with
Sc, page 125)*; ch 3, (sc, ch 3, sc) in next Shell (ch-2
sp), ch 3, sc in ch-1 sp between Shells, ch 3, (sc, ch 3,
sc) in next Shell, † ch 5, decrease, ch 5, (sc, ch 3, sc)
in next Shell †, repeat from † to † 22 times **more**,
[ch 3, sc in sp between Shells, ch 3, (sc, ch 3, sc) in
next Shell] twice, repeat from † to † across, ch 3; join
with slip st to first sc, finish off.

SECOND STRIP
Work same as First Strip through Rnd 1 of Edging.
Rnd 2 (Joining rnd)**:** With **right** side facing, join
Color A with sc in sp before Shell at end of Strip;
ch 3, (sc, ch 3, sc) in next Shell, ch 3, sc in ch-1 sp
between Shells, ch 3, (sc, ch 3, sc) in next Shell,
† ch 5, decrease, ch 5, (sc, ch 3, sc) in next Shell †,
repeat from † to † 22 times **more**, ch 3, sc in sp
between Shells, ch 3, (sc, ch 3, sc) in next Shell, ch 3,
sc in sp between Shells, ch 3, sc in next Shell, ch 1,
with **right** side of **previous Strip** facing, drop loop
from hook, insert hook in second ch of corresponding
ch-3 on **previous Strip**, hook dropped loop and
draw through, ch 1, sc in same sp on **new Strip**,
★ ch 2, drop loop from hook, insert hook in third ch
of next ch-5 loop on **previous Strip**, hook dropped
loop and draw through, ch 2, decrease on **new Strip**,
ch 2, drop loop from hook, insert hook in third ch of
next ch-5 loop on **previous Strip**, hook dropped
loop and draw through, ch 2, sc in next Shell on **new
Strip**, ch 1, drop loop from hook, insert hook in
second ch of next ch-3 on **previous Strip**, hook
dropped loop and draw through, ch 1, sc in same sp
on new Strip; repeat from ★ across, ch 1, hdc in first
sc to form last sp; finish off.

Repeat Second Strip for a total of 10 Strips; do **not**
finish off at end of last Strip.

BORDER

Rnd 1: Ch 1, sc in same sp, ch 3, sc in next ch-3 sp, ch 3, (sc, ch 3, sc) in next ch-3 sp (point), ch 3, (sc in next sp, ch 3) across to ch-3 sp on next point, (sc, ch 3, sc) in ch-3 sp, † (ch 3, sc in next ch-3 sp) twice, ch 1, sc in next ch-1 sp to **right** of joining, ch 1, sc in next ch-1 sp to **left** of joining, ch 1, (sc in next ch-3 sp, ch 3) twice, (sc, ch 3, sc) in next ch-3 sp (point) †, repeat from † to † 8 times **more**, ch 3, (sc in next sp, ch 3) across to ch-3 sp on next point, (sc, ch 3, sc) in ch-3 sp, repeat from † to † 8 times, (ch 3, sc in next ch-3 sp) twice, ch 1, sc in next ch-1 sp to **right** of joining, ch 1, sc in next ch-1 sp to **left** of joining, sc in first sc to form last sp.

Rnd 2: Slip st in same sp, work Picot, (slip st in next sp, work Picot) 3 times, slip st in same sp, work Picot, (slip st in next sp, work Picot) across through next point, † slip st in same sp, work Picot, (slip st in next sp, work Picot) 3 times, skip next ch-1 sp, (slip st in next sp, work Picot) 4 times †, repeat from † to † 8 times **more**, slip st in same sp, work Picot, (slip st in next sp, work Picot) across through next point, repeat from † to † 8 times, slip st in same sp, work Picot, (slip st in next sp, work Picot) 3 times, skip next ch-1 sp; join with slip st to first slip st, finish off.

7

gingham checks

This throw is brimming with country style! The afghan is fashioned with worsted weight yarn in white and shades of peach to create the look of gingham checks. A flouncy ruffle adds a sweet finish.

Finished Size: Approximately 34" x 41"

MATERIALS
Worsted Weight Yarn, approximately:
Color A (Light Peach) - 11 ounces,
(310 grams, 775 yards)
Color B (Peach) - 6 ounces,
(170 grams, 420 yards)
Color C (White) - 9 ounces,
(260 grams, 635 yards)
Crochet hook, size I (5.50 mm) **or** size needed
for gauge
Yarn needle

GAUGE: Each Square = 3½"

SQUARE
(Make 49 with Color A, 30 with Color B, and 20 with Color C)
Ch 6; join with slip st to form a ring.
Rnd 1 (Right side)**:** Ch 3 **(counts as first dc, now and throughout)**, 2 dc in ring, (ch 2, 3 dc in ring) 3 times, ch 1, hdc in first dc to form last sp: 12 dc.
Note: Loop a short piece of yarn around any stitch to mark last round as **right** side.
Rnd 2: Ch 3, 2 dc in same sp, ch 1, ★ (3 dc, ch 2, 3 dc) in next ch-2 sp, ch 1; repeat from ★ around, 3 dc in same sp as beginning ch-3, hdc in first dc to form last sp: 24 dc.
Rnd 3: Ch 3, (2 dc, ch 2, 3 dc) in same sp, ch 1, 3 dc in next ch-1 sp, ch 1, ★ (3 dc, ch 2, 3 dc) in next corner ch-2 sp, ch 1, 3 dc in next ch-1 sp, ch 1; repeat from ★ around; join with slip st to first dc, finish off: 36 dc.

ASSEMBLY
With **wrong** sides together and Color A, and working through **both** loops, whipstitch Squares together, forming 5 vertical strips of 11 Squares each, in the following order: Color B, (Color A, Color B) 5 times, beginning in second ch of first corner and ending in first ch of next corner **(Fig. 25a, page 126)**. Whipstitch remaining Squares together, forming 4 vertical strips of 11 Squares each, in the following order: Color A, (Color C, Color A) 5 times; then whipstitch strips together, alternating colors.

RUFFLE
Rnd 1: With **right** side facing, join Color C with slip st in any corner ch-2 sp; ch 1, 3 sc in same sp, sc in each dc and in each ch around working 3 sc in each corner ch-2 sp; join with slip st to first sc: 524 sc.
Rnd 2: Turn; slip st in next sc, ch 1, sc in same st, ch 1, skip next sc, (sc in next sc, ch 1, skip next sc) around; join with slip st to first sc: 262 ch-1 sps.
Rnd 3: Turn; slip st in first ch-1 sp, ch 3, (dc, ch 2, 2 dc) in same sp, (2 dc, ch 2, 2 dc) in next ch-1 sp and in each ch-1 sp around; join with slip st to first dc, finish off.

*Worked in quick-to-finish squares of worsted weight yarn,
this pretty afghan is a breeze to whip together! Each dreamy
motif features a tiny "cloud" drifting in the center.*

Finished Size: Approximately 39" x 46"

MATERIALS
Worsted Weight Yarn, approximately:
   MC (White) - 15 ounces,
      (430 grams, 985 yards)
   CC (Blue) - 13 ounces, (370 grams, 855 yards)
Crochet hook, size I (5.50 mm) **or** size needed for
   gauge
Yarn needle

GAUGE: Each Square = 6½"

SQUARE (Make 42)
Rnd 1 (Right side)**:** With MC, ch 5, (3 dc, ch 1) 3
times in fifth ch from hook, 2 dc in same ch; join with
slip st to fourth ch of beginning ch-5: 4 ch-1 sps.
Note: Loop a short piece of yarn around any stitch to
mark last round as **right** side.
Rnd 2: Slip st in first ch-1 sp, ch 7, (slip st in next
ch-1 sp, ch 7) around; join with slip st to first st:
4 loops.
Rnd 3: Slip st in first loop, ch 3 **(counts as first
dc, now and throughout)**, (3 dc, ch 2, 4 dc) in
same loop, ch 1, ★ (4 dc, ch 2, 4 dc) in next loop,
ch 1; repeat from ★ around; join with slip st to first dc,
finish off: 32 dc.
Rnd 4: With **right** side facing, join CC with sc in any
ch-2 sp **(see Joining with Sc, page 125)**; ch 1, sc
in same sp, sc in next 3 dc, skip next dc, (dc, ch 1, dc)
in next ch-1 sp, skip next dc, sc in next 3 dc, ★ (sc,
ch 1, sc) in next ch-2 sp, sc in next 3 dc, skip next dc,
(dc, ch 1, dc) in next ch-1 sp, skip next dc, sc in next
3 dc; repeat from ★ around; join with slip st to first sc.

Rnd 5: Ch 3, (2 dc, ch 1, 2 dc) in next ch-1 sp, dc in
next 5 sts, sc in next ch-1 sp, ★ dc in next 5 sts, (2 dc,
ch 1, 2 dc) in next ch-1 sp, dc in next 5 sts, sc in next
ch-1 sp; repeat from ★ around to last 4 sts, dc in last
4 sts; join with slip st to first dc, finish off: 56 dc.
Rnd 6: With **right** side facing, join MC with slip st in
any corner ch-1 sp; ch 3, (dc, ch 1, 2 dc) in same sp,
(skip next dc, 2 dc in next st) 7 times, skip next st,
★ (2 dc, ch 1, 2 dc) in next ch-1 sp, (skip next dc, 2 dc
in next st) 7 times, skip next st; repeat from ★ around;
join with slip st to first dc, finish off: 72 dc.
Rnd 7: With **right** side facing, join CC with slip st in
any corner ch-1 sp; ch 3, (dc, ch 1, 2 dc) in same sp,
2 sc in sp **between** each 2-dc group across to next
corner ch-1 sp, ★ (2 dc, ch 1, 2 dc) in ch-1 sp, 2 sc in
sp **between** each 2-dc group across to next corner
ch-1 sp; repeat from ★ around; join with slip st to first
dc, finish off.

ASSEMBLY
With **wrong** sides together and CC, and working
through **inside** loops only, whipstitch Squares
together forming 6 vertical strips of 7 Squares each
(Fig. 25b, page 126); then whipstitch strips together,
securing seam at each joining.

FRINGE
Using 4, 12" strands of MC, add fringe in every other
stitch across each end of Afghan **(Figs. 26a & b,
page 126)**.

11

granny's love

A kaleidoscope of soft hues creates this keepsake throw featuring tiny granny squares. Strips of the squares are edged with a contrasting color, whipstitched together, and finished with a coordinating border.

Finished Size: Approximately 37" x 42"

MATERIALS

Sport Weight Yarn, approximately:
  MC (White) - 12 ounces,
    (340 grams, 1,130 yards)
  Color A (Blue) - 1 ounce, (30 grams, 95 yards)
  Color B (Yellow) - 1 ounce,
    (30 grams, 95 yards)
  Color C (Pink) - 1 ounce, (30 grams, 95 yards)
  Color D (Green) - 1 ounce,
    (30 grams, 95 yards)
Crochet hook, size F (3.75 mm) **or** size needed
  for gauge
Yarn needle

GAUGE: Each Square = 2¹/₂"
        Each Strip = 5" x 40"

STRIP A

SQUARE A (Make 30)

Rnd 1 (Right side): With Color A, ch 4, 2 dc in fourth ch from hook, ch 3, (3 dc in same st, ch 3) 3 times; join with slip st to top of beginning ch, finish off.

Note: Loop a short piece of yarn around any stitch to mark last round as **right** side.

Rnd 2: With **right** side facing, join MC with slip st in any ch-3 sp; ch 3 **(counts as first dc, now and throughout)**, (2 dc, ch 3, 3 dc) in same sp, ch 1, ★ (3 dc, ch 3, 3 dc) in next ch-3 sp, ch 1; repeat from ★ around; join with slip st to first dc, finish off.

JOINING

With **wrong** sides together and MC, and working through **both** loops, whipstitch Squares together forming 2 vertical Strips of 15 Squares each **(Fig. 25a, page 126)**; do **not** join Strips.

EDGING

Rnd 1: With **right** side facing, join MC with sc in top **right** ch-3 sp **(see Joining with Sc, page 125)**; ch 3, sc in same sp, † ch 1, skip next dc, sc in next dc, ch 1, sc in next ch-1 sp, ch 1, skip next dc, sc in next dc, ch 1, (sc, ch 3, sc) in next ch-3 sp, ch 1, skip next dc, sc in next dc, ch 1, sc in next ch-1 sp, ch 1, skip next dc, sc in next dc, ch 1, **[**(sc in next sp, ch 1) twice, skip next dc, sc in next dc, ch 1, sc in next ch-1 sp, ch 1, skip next dc, sc in next dc, ch 1**]** across to next ch-3 sp †, (sc, ch 3, sc) in ch-3 sp, repeat from † to † once; join with slip st to first sc: 160 sps.

Rnd 2: Slip st in first ch-3 sp, ch 1, (sc, ch 3, sc) in same sp, ch 1, (sc in next ch-1 sp, ch 1) across to next ch-3 sp, ★ (sc, ch 3, sc) in ch-3 sp, ch 1, (sc in next ch-1 sp, ch 1) across to next ch-3 sp; repeat from ★ around; join with slip st to first sc, finish off: 164 sps.

Rnd 3: With **right** side facing, join Color B with slip st in top **right** ch-3 sp; ch 3, (2 dc, ch 3, 3 dc) in same sp, ch 1, skip next ch-1 sp, (3 dc in next ch-1 sp, ch 1, skip next ch-1 sp) across to next ch-3 sp, ★ (3 dc, ch 3, 3 dc) in ch-3 sp, ch 1, skip next ch-1 sp, (3 dc in next ch-1 sp, ch 1, skip next ch-1 sp) across to next ch-3 sp; repeat from ★ around; join with slip st to first dc, finish off.

Rnd 4: With **right** side facing, join MC with slip st in any ch-3 sp; ch 3, (2 dc, ch 3, 3 dc) in same sp, ch 1, (3 dc in next ch-1 sp, ch 1) across to next ch-3 sp, ★ (3 dc, ch 3, 3 dc) in ch-3 sp, ch 1, (3 dc in next ch-1 sp, ch 1) across to next ch-3 sp; repeat from ★ around; join with slip st to first dc, finish off.
Repeat for second Strip.

STRIP B

SQUARE B (Make 30)

Work same as Square A working in the following color sequence: 1 Rnd each of Color C and MC.

JOINING

Work same as Strip A.

EDGING
Work same as Strip A working in the following color sequence: 2 Rnds MC, 1 rnd each of Color D and MC.

STRIP C
SQUARE C (Make 30)
Work same as Square A working in the following color sequence: 1 Rnd each of Color B and MC.

JOINING
Work same as Strip A.

EDGING
Work same as Strip A working in the following color sequence: 2 Rnds MC, 1 rnd each of Color A and MC.

STRIP D
SQUARE D (Make 15)
Work same as Square A working in the following color sequence: 1 Rnd each of Color D and MC.

JOINING
Work same as Strip A forming 1 vertical Strip.

EDGING
Work same as Strip A working in the following color sequence: 2 Rnds MC, 1 rnd each of Color C and MC.

ASSEMBLY
Whipstitch Strips together in same manner as joining, in the following order: A-B-C-D-A-B-C.

BORDER

Rnd 1: With **right** side facing, join MC with sc in top right ch-3 sp; ch 3, sc in same sp, ch 1, † skip next dc, sc in next dc, ch 1, (sc in next ch-1 sp, ch 1, skip next dc, sc in next dc, ch 1) 4 times, ★ (sc in next sp, ch 1) twice, skip next dc, sc in next dc, ch 1, (sc in next ch-1 sp, ch 1, skip next dc, sc in next dc, ch 1) 4 times; repeat from ★ across to next ch-3 sp, (sc, ch 3, sc) in ch-3 sp, ch 1, skip next dc, sc in next dc, ch 1, (sc in next ch-1 sp, ch 1, skip next dc, sc in next dc, ch 1) across to next ch-3 sp †, (sc, ch 3, sc) in ch-3 sp, ch 1, repeat from † to † once; join with slip st to first sc.

Rnd 2: Slip st in first ch-3 sp, ch 1, (sc, ch 3, sc) in same sp, ch 1, (sc in next ch-1 sp, ch 1) across to next ch-3 sp, ★ (sc, ch 3, sc) in ch-3 sp, ch 1, (sc in next ch-1 sp, ch 1) across to next ch-3 sp; repeat from ★ around; join with slip st to first sc.

To work **Corner Lace St**, sc in sp indicated, ch 4, dc in fourth ch from hook, sc in same sp.

To work **Lace St**, ch 3, dc in third ch from hook.

Rnd 3: Slip st in first ch-3 sp, ch 1, work Corner Lace St in same sp, work Lace St, skip next ch-1 sp, (sc in next ch-1 sp, work Lace St, skip next ch-1 sp) across to next ch-3 sp, ★ work Corner Lace St in ch-3 sp, work Lace St, skip next ch-1 sp, (sc in next ch-1 sp, work Lace St, skip next ch-1 sp) across to next ch-3 sp; repeat from ★ around; join with slip st to first sc, finish off.

peppermint wrapper

Lacy white rows made up of double crochets and V-stitches alternate with bands of red V-stitches to form this peppermint-striped wrap. For a festive finish, chain loops accent the edges of our Yuletide afghan.

Finished Size: Approximately 36" x 43"

MATERIALS
Worsted Weight Yarn, approximately:
   MC (White) - 19 ounces,
     (540 grams, 1,110 yards)
   CC (Red) - 5 ounces, (140 grams, 295 yards)
Crochet hook, size H (5.00 mm) **or** size needed for gauge

GAUGE: 15 dc and 8 rows = 4"

STRIPE SEQUENCE
Work 5 rows MC, ★ 1 row CC, 5 rows MC; repeat from ★ throughout *(Fig. 21a, page 125)*.

BODY
With MC, ch 130 **loosely**.

Row 1 (Right side): Dc in fourth ch from hook and in each ch across: 128 sts.

Note: Loop a short piece of yarn around any stitch to mark last row as **right** side.

To work **V-St**, (dc, ch 1, dc) in dc indicated.

Row 2: Ch 3 **(counts as first dc, now and throughout)**, turn; skip next dc, work V-St in next dc, (skip next 2 dc, work V-St in next dc) across to last 2 sts, skip last dc, dc in top of beginning ch: 42 ch-1 sps.

Row 3: Ch 3, turn; dc in next dc and in each ch-1 sp and each dc across: 128 dc.

Rows 4-83: Repeat Rows 2 and 3, 40 times. Finish off.

EDGING

Rnd 1: With **right** side facing, join CC with slip st in first dc on last row; ch 1, 3 sc in same st, sc in each dc across to last dc, 3 sc in last dc; work 156 sc evenly spaced across end of rows to beginning ch; working in free loops of beginning ch *(Fig. 23b, page 125)*, 3 sc in first ch, sc in each ch across to next corner ch, 3 sc in corner ch; work 156 sc evenly spaced across end of rows; join with slip st to first sc: 576 sc.

Rnd 2: Ch 4, skip next sc, (slip st in next sc, ch 4, skip next sc) around; join with slip st in same st as joining, finish off.

ruffles all around

Double ruffles and satin ribbon add fanciful touches to this blanket of shell stitches. Destined to become a cherished keepsake, the frilly wrap is ideal for baby's homecoming, christening, or other outing.

Finished Size: Approximately 32" x 36"

MATERIALS
Baby Yarn, approximately:
MC (White) - 16 ounces,
(450 grams, 1,790 yards)
CC (Green) - 7¾ ounces,
(220 grams, 870 yards)
Crochet hook, size F (3.75 mm) **or** size needed for gauge
7 yards of ¼" wide satin ribbon
Tapestry needle
Sewing needle and thread to match ribbon

GAUGE: In pattern, (5-dc group, 2 dc) 3 times and 10 rows = 4"

BODY
With MC, ch 125 **loosely**.
Row 1: Dc in eighth ch from hook, (ch 2, skip next 2 chs, dc in next ch) across: 40 sps.
Row 2 (Right side): Ch 5 **(counts as first dc plus ch 2, now and throughout)**, turn; dc in next dc, 5 dc in next dc, ★ 2 dc in next dc, 5 dc in next dc; repeat from ★ across to last dc, dc in last dc, ch 2, skip next 2 chs, dc in next ch: 19 5-dc groups.
Note: Loop a short piece of yarn around any stitch to mark last row as **right** side.
Row 3: Ch 5, turn; dc in next dc, skip next 2 dc, dc in sp **before** next dc, skip next dc, dc in sp **before** next dc, ★ skip next 3 dc, 5 dc in sp **before** next dc, skip next 3 dc, dc in sp **before** next dc, skip next dc, dc in sp **before** next dc; repeat from ★ across to last 4 dc, skip next 2 dc, dc in next dc, ch 2, dc in last dc: 18 5-dc groups.
Row 4: Ch 5, turn; dc in next dc, skip next dc, 5 dc in sp **before** next dc, ★ skip next 3 dc, dc in sp **before** next dc, skip next dc, dc in sp **before** next dc, skip next 3 dc, 5 dc in sp **before** next dc; repeat from ★ across to last 3 dc, skip next dc, dc in next dc, ch 2, dc in last dc: 19 5-dc groups.
Rows 5-73: Repeat Rows 3 and 4, 34 times, then repeat Row 3 once **more**.

Row 74: Ch 5, turn; dc in next dc, ch 2, skip next dc, dc in sp **before** next dc, ★ ch 2, skip next 3 dc, dc in next dc, ch 2, skip next 3 dc, dc in sp **before** next dc; repeat from ★ across to last 3 dc, ch 2, skip next dc, dc in next dc, place marker around dc just made to mark Second Ruffle placement, ch 2, dc in last dc, finish off: 40 sps.

FIRST RUFFLE
Rnd 1: With **right** side facing, join CC with slip st in last ch-2 sp on last row; ch 3 **(counts as first dc, now and throughout)**, 2 dc in same sp, (ch 1, 3 dc) twice in same sp, (ch 1, 2 dc) in end of each row across to next corner sp, (ch 1, 3 dc) 3 times in corner sp; working over skipped chs of beginning ch, (ch 1, 2 dc) in each sp across to next corner sp, (ch 1, 3 dc) 3 times in corner sp; (ch 1, 2 dc) in end of each row across to next corner sp, (ch 1, 3 dc) 3 times in corner sp, ch 1, (2 dc, ch 1) in each ch-2 sp across; join with slip st to first dc.
Rnd 2: Ch 3, 3 dc in next dc, (dc in next 2 dc, 3 dc in next dc) twice, dc in next dc, ★ 2 dc in next dc and in each dc across to next 3-dc group, dc in next dc, 3 dc in next dc, (dc in next 2 dc, 3 dc in next dc) twice, dc in next dc; repeat from ★ 2 times **more**, 2 dc in next dc and in each dc across; join with slip st to first dc.
Rnds 3-5: Ch 3, dc in next dc and in each dc around; join with slip st to first dc.
Rnd 6: Ch 1, sc in same st, ch 3, slip st in third ch from hook, skip next dc, ★ sc in next dc, ch 3, slip st in third ch from hook, skip next dc; repeat from ★ around; join with slip st to first sc, finish off.

SECOND RUFFLE
Rnd 1: With **right** side facing, and working in **front** of First Ruffle, join MC with slip st around post of marked dc *(Fig. 11, page 123)*; ch 1, sc around post of same st, ch 3, (sc around ch-2 at end of next row, ch 3) across; (sc around post of next dc, ch 3) across, (sc around ch-2 at end of next row, ch 3) across, (sc around post of next dc, ch 3) across; join with slip st to first sc.

Rnd 2: Slip st in first ch-3 sp, ch 3, 2 dc in same sp, (ch 1, 3 dc) twice in same sp, ch 1, ★ (2 dc, ch 1) in each ch-3 sp across to next corner ch-3 sp, (3 dc, ch 1) 3 times in corner sp; repeat from ★ 2 times **more**, (2 dc, ch 1) in each ch-3 sp across; join with slip st to first dc.

Rnd 3: Ch 3, 3 dc in next dc, (dc in next 2 dc, 3 dc in next dc) twice, dc in next dc, ★ 2 dc in next dc and in each dc across to next 3-dc group, dc in next dc, 3 dc in next dc, (dc in next 2 dc, 3 dc in next dc) twice, dc in next dc; repeat from ★ 2 times **more**, 2 dc in next dc and in each dc across; join with slip st to first dc.

Rnd 4: Ch 3, dc in next dc and in each dc around; join with slip st to first dc.

Rnd 5: Ch 1, sc in same st, ch 3, slip st in third ch from hook, skip next dc, ★ sc in next dc, ch 3, slip st in third ch from hook, skip next dc; repeat from ★ around; join with slip st to first sc, finish off.

FINISHING

With **right** side facing and leaving a 10" end at beginning, weave ribbon through sps along each edge of Afghan; tie ends in a bow at each corner. Tack bows to Afghan to secure and trim as desired.

cozy whisper

Variegated yarn brings a whisper of color to the rows of clusters on this cozy afghan. Worked across the length of the throw, the wide textured stripes are separated by airy mesh rows.

Finished Size: Approximately 35" x 47"

MATERIALS
Sport Weight Yarn, approximately:
   MC (White) - 12 ounces,
     (340 grams, 1,210 yards)
   CC (Variegated) - 7 ounces,
     (200 grams, 705 yards)
Crochet hook, size G (4.00 mm) **or** size needed
   for gauge

GAUGE: In pattern, 17 sts = 4"
          and 13 rows = 4¼"

STRIPE SEQUENCE
(1 Row MC, 1 row CC) 3 times, 5 rows MC, ★ 1 row CC, (1 row MC, 1 row CC) twice, 5 rows MC; repeat from ★ 8 times **more (Fig. 21a, page 125)**.

Note: Each row is worked across length of Afghan.

BODY
With MC, ch 201 **loosely**.
Row 1 (Right side): Dc in fourth ch from hook **(3 skipped chs count as first dc)** and in each ch across: 199 dc.
Note: Loop a short piece of yarn around any stitch to mark last row as **right** side.
To work **Cluster**, ★ YO, insert hook in Back Loop Only of dc indicated **(Fig. 22, page 125)**, YO and pull up a loop, YO and draw through 2 loops on hook; repeat from ★ 3 times **more**, YO and draw through all 5 loops on hook **(Figs. 14a & b, page 123)**.
Row 2: Ch 1, turn; sc in first 3 dc, work Cluster in next dc, (sc in next 5 dc, work Cluster in next dc) across to last 3 dc, sc in last 3 dc: 33 Clusters.
Row 3: Ch 3 **(counts as first dc, now and throughout)**, turn; dc in next sc and in each st across: 199 dc.

Row 4: Ch 1, turn; sc in first 6 dc, work Cluster in next dc, (sc in next 5 dc, work Cluster in next dc) across to last 6 dc, sc in last 6 dc: 32 Clusters.
Row 5: Ch 3, turn; dc in next sc and in each st across: 199 dc.
Row 6: Ch 1, turn; sc in first 3 dc, work Cluster in next dc, (sc in next 5 dc, work Cluster in next dc) across to last 3 dc, sc in last 3 dc: 33 Clusters.
Row 7: Ch 3, turn; dc in next sc and in each st across: 199 dc.
Row 8: Ch 1, turn; sc in each dc across.
Row 9: Ch 4 **(counts as first dc plus ch 1, now and throughout)**, turn; skip next sc, dc in next sc, (ch 1, skip next sc, dc in next sc) across: 100 dc and 99 ch-1 sps.
Row 10: Ch 1, turn; sc in each dc and in each ch-1 sp across: 199 sc.
Row 11: Ch 3, turn; dc in next sc and in each sc across.
Rows 12-100: Repeat Rows 2-11, 8 times; then repeat Rows 2-10 once **more**.
Row 101: Ch 1, turn; slip st in first sc, (ch 1, skip next sc, slip st in next sc) across; finish off.

EDGING
Row 1: With **wrong** side facing and working in free loops of beginning ch **(Fig. 23b, page 125)**, join MC with sc in ch at base of first dc **(see Joining with Sc, page 125)**; sc in each ch across: 199 sc.
Row 2: Ch 4, turn; skip next sc, dc in next sc, (ch 1, skip next sc, dc in next sc) across: 100 dc and 99 ch-1 sps.
Row 3: Ch 1, turn; sc in each dc and in each ch-1 sp across: 199 sc.
Row 4: Ch 1, turn; slip st in first sc, (ch 1, skip next sc, slip st in next sc) across; finish off.

FRINGE
Using three 10" lengths of corresponding color, add fringe to end of each row on Afghan **(Figs. 26c & d, page 126)**.

cuddletime blossoms

Cushy blossoms of pink and white puff stitches transform this dainty afghan into a sweet bouquet for baby. Worked in squares and finished with an openwork edging, the wrap is sure to become a cherished favorite.

Finished Size: Approximately 31" x 37"

MATERIALS
Sport Weight Yarn, approximately:
  MC (White) - 9½ ounces,
    (270 grams, 895 yards)
  CC (Pink) - 7 ounces,
    (200 grams, 660 yards)
Crochet hook, size F (3.75 mm) **or** size needed
  for gauge
Yarn needle

GAUGE: Each Square = 3¼"

SQUARE A (Make 50)
With CC, ch 4; join with slip st to form a ring.
Rnd 1 (Right side)**:** Ch 1, 8 sc in ring; join with slip st to first sc.
Note: Loop a short piece of yarn around any stitch to mark last round as **right** side.

To work **Puff St**, ★ YO, insert hook in st indicated, YO and pull up a ½" loop; repeat from ★ 3 times **more**, YO and draw through all 9 loops on hook *(Fig. 17, page 123)*.
Rnd 2: Pull up loop on hook to measure ½", work Puff St in same st, (ch 3, work Puff St in next sc) around, ch 1, hdc in top of first Puff St to form last ch-3 sp: 8 Puff Sts.
Rnd 3: Ch 3 **(counts as first dc, now and throughout)**, 2 dc in same sp, 3 dc in next ch-3 sp, ★ (3 dc, ch 2, 3 dc) in next ch-3 sp, 3 dc in next ch-3 sp; repeat from ★ 2 times **more**, 3 dc in same sp as first dc, ch 2; join with slip st to first dc, finish off: 36 dc.
Rnd 4: With **right** side facing, join MC with slip st in any ch-2 sp; ch 3, 2 dc in same sp, dc in next 9 dc, ★ (3 dc, ch 2, 3 dc) in next ch-2 sp, dc in next 9 dc; repeat from ★ 2 times **more**, 3 dc in same sp as first dc, ch 2; join with slip st to first dc, finish off: 60 dc.

SQUARE B (Make 49)
With MC, ch 4; join with slip st to form a ring.
Rnd 1 (Right side)**:** Ch 1, 8 sc in ring; join with slip st to first sc.
Note: Mark last round as **right** side.
Rnd 2: Pull up loop on hook to measure ½", work Puff St in same st, ch 3, (work Puff St in next sc, ch 3) around; join with slip st to top of first Puff St, finish off: 8 Puff Sts.
Rnd 3: With **right** side facing, join CC with slip st in any ch-3 sp; ch 3, 2 dc in same sp, 3 dc in next ch-3 sp, ★ (3 dc, ch 2, 3 dc) in next ch-3 sp, 3 dc in next ch-3 sp; repeat from ★ 2 times **more**, 3 dc in same sp as first dc, ch 2; join with slip st to first dc, finish off: 36 dc.
Rnd 4: With **right** side facing, join MC with slip st in any ch-2 sp; ch 3, 2 dc in same sp, dc in next 9 dc, ★ (3 dc, ch 2, 3 dc) in next ch-2 sp, dc in next 9 dc; repeat from ★ 2 times **more**, 3 dc in same sp as first dc, ch 2; join with slip st to first dc, finish off: 60 dc.

ASSEMBLY

With **wrong** sides together and MC, and working through **inside** loops only, whipstitch Squares together forming 9 vertical strips of 11 Squares each following Placement Diagram *(Fig. 25b, page 126)*; then whipstitch strips together securing seam at each joining.

PLACEMENT DIAGRAM

A	B	A	B	A	B	A	B	A
B	A	B	A	B	A	B	A	B
A	B	A	B	A	B	A	B	A
B	A	B	A	B	A	B	A	B
A	B	A	B	A	B	A	B	A
B	A	B	A	B	A	B	A	B
A	B	A	B	A	B	A	B	A
B	A	B	A	B	A	B	A	B
A	B	A	B	A	B	A	B	A
B	A	B	A	B	A	B	A	B
A	B	A	B	A	B	A	B	A

EDGING

Rnd 1: With **right** side facing, join CC with slip st in any corner ch-2 sp; ch 4, (dc, ch 1) twice in same sp, ★ † skip next dc, (dc in next dc, ch 1, skip next dc) 7 times, **[**(dc in next sp, ch 1) twice, skip next dc, (dc in next dc, ch 1, skip next dc) 7 times**]** across to next corner ch-2 sp †, (dc, ch 1) 3 times in corner ch-2 sp; repeat from ★ 2 times **more**, then repeat from † to † once; join with slip st to third ch of beginning ch-4.

Rnd 2: (Slip st, ch 1, hdc) in first ch-1 sp, ch 1; working from **left** to **right**, ★ work reverse hdc in next ch-1 sp *(Figs. 19a-d, page 124)*, ch 1; repeat from ★ around; join with slip st to first hdc, finish off.

diamond trellis

Our dazzling baby afghan shows that diamonds really are a girl's best friend!
Finished with a scalloped edging, this blanket of lacy diamonds is created
with a pattern of plush shells mingled among the meshwork.

Finished Size: Approximately 34" x 47"

MATERIALS

Sport Weight Yarn, approximately:
   19 ounces, (540 grams, 1,790 yards)
Crochet hook, size G (4.00 mm) **or** size needed
   for gauge

GAUGE: 17 dc and 9 rows = 4"

BODY

Ch 150 **loosely**.

Row 1 (Right side)**:** Sc in second ch from hook,
(ch 5, skip next 3 chs, sc in next ch) twice, skip next
ch, 5 dc in next ch **(Shell made)**, skip next ch, sc in
next ch, ★ (ch 5, skip next 3 chs, sc in next ch) 3
times, skip next ch, work Shell in next ch, skip next
ch, sc in next ch; repeat from ★ across to last 8 chs,
(ch 5, skip next 3 chs, sc in next ch) twice: 9 Shells.

Row 2: Ch 5, turn; sc in first loop, ch 5, sc in next
loop, work Shell in next sc, skip next 2 dc, sc in next
dc, work Shell in next sc, sc in next loop, ★ (ch 5, sc
in next loop) twice, work Shell in next sc, skip next
2 dc, sc in next dc, work Shell in next sc, sc in next
loop; repeat from ★ across to last loop, ch 5, sc in last
loop, ch 2, dc in last sc: 18 Shells.

Row 3: Ch 1, turn; sc in first dc, ch 5, ★ sc in next
loop, work Shell in next sc, skip next 2 dc, sc in next
dc, ch 5, skip next 5 sts, sc in next dc, work Shell in
next sc, sc in next loop, ch 5; repeat from ★ across to
last loop, skip next sc and next 2 chs, sc in next ch.

Row 4: Ch 3 **(counts as first dc, now and
throughout)**, turn; 2 dc in same st, sc in first loop,
★ work Shell in next sc, skip next 2 dc, sc in next dc,
ch 5, sc in next loop, ch 5, skip next 2 dc, sc in next
dc, work Shell in next sc, sc in next loop; repeat from
★ across to last sc, 3 dc in last sc.

Row 5: Ch 1, turn; sc in first dc, work Shell in next
sc, ★ skip next 2 dc, sc in next dc, ch 5, (sc in next
loop, ch 5) twice, skip next 2 dc, sc in next dc, work
Shell in next sc; repeat from ★ across to last 3 dc, skip
next 2 dc, sc in last dc: 10 Shells.

Row 6: Ch 3, turn; 2 dc in same st, skip next 2 dc,
sc in next dc, ★ work Shell in next sc, sc in next loop,
(ch 5, sc in next loop) twice, work Shell in next sc,
skip next 2 dc, sc in next dc; repeat from ★ across to
last 3 sts, skip next 2 dc, 3 dc in last sc: 18 Shells.

Row 7: Ch 1, turn; sc in first dc, ch 5, skip next
5 sts, sc in next dc, ★ work Shell in next sc, sc in next
loop, ch 5, sc in next loop, work Shell in next sc, skip
next 2 dc, sc in next dc, ch 5, skip next 5 sts, sc in
next dc; repeat from ★ across.

Row 8: Ch 5, turn; sc in first loop, ★ ch 5, skip next
2 dc, sc in next dc, work Shell in next sc, sc in next
loop, work Shell in next sc, skip next 2 dc, sc in next
dc, ch 5, sc in next loop; repeat from ★ across to last
sc, ch 2, dc in last sc.

Row 9: Ch 1, turn; sc in first dc, ch 5, sc in next
loop, ch 5, skip next 2 dc, sc in next dc, work Shell in
next sc, skip next 2 dc, sc in next dc, ch 5, ★ (sc in
next loop, ch 5) twice, skip next 2 dc, sc in next dc,
work Shell in next sc, skip next 2 dc, sc in next dc,
ch 5; repeat from ★ across to last 2 loops, sc in next
loop, ch 5, skip next sc and next 2 chs, sc in next ch:
9 Shells.

Repeat Rows 2-9 until Afghan measures
approximately 46", ending by working Row 9; do **not**
finish off.

EDGING

Rnd 1: Ch 1, do **not** turn; work 192 sc evenly
spaced across end of rows; working in free loops of
beginning ch *(Fig. 23b, page 125)*, 3 sc in first ch,
work 147 sc evenly spaced across to next corner ch,
3 sc in corner ch; work 192 sc evenly spaced across
end of rows; working across sts on last row, 3 sc in
first sc, work 147 sc evenly spaced across to last sc,
3 sc in last sc; join with slip st to first sc: 690 sc.

Rnd 2: Ch 3, dc in same st, skip next 2 sc, ★ slip st
in next sc, ch 3, dc in same st, skip next 2 sc; repeat
from ★ around; join with slip st in st at base of
beginning ch-3, finish off.

daisies for baby

A chain of delicate daisies blooms in the center of each strip of this sweet mile-a-minute baby afghan. It's perfect for adding a summery touch to the nursery.

Finished Size: Approximately 30" x 44"

MATERIALS
Sport Weight Yarn, approximately:
MC (White) - 8 ounces, (230 grams, 755 yards)
Color A (Yellow) - 5 ounces,
 (140 grams, 470 yards)
Color B (Green) - 3 ounces,
 (90 grams, 285 yards)
Crochet hook, size H (5.00 mm) **or** size needed
 for gauge

GAUGE: 16 dc = 4"
 One Strip = 5" wide

FIRST STRIP
With Color B, ch 177 **loosely**.
Foundation Row (Right side): Sc in second ch from hook and in each ch across; finish off: 176 sc.
Note: Loop a short piece of yarn around any stitch to mark last row as **right** side.
To work **Cluster**, ★ YO twice, insert hook in st or sp indicated, YO and pull up a loop, (YO and draw through 2 loops on hook) twice; repeat from ★ 2 times **more**, YO and draw through all 4 loops on hook *(Figs. 14a & b, page 123)*.
Rnd 1 (Daisy): With **right** side facing, join Color A with slip st in first sc; ch 3, ★ YO twice, insert hook in same st, YO and pull up a loop, (YO and draw through 2 loops on hook) twice; repeat from ★ once **more**, YO and draw through all 3 loops on hook **(beginning Cluster made)**, (ch 3, work Cluster in same st) 5 times, skip next 6 sc, [work Cluster in next sc, (ch 3, work Cluster in same st) twice, skip next 6 sc] across to last sc, work Cluster in last sc, (ch 3, work Cluster in same st) 5 times; working in each sp formed by Cluster groups, [work Cluster in next sp *(Fig. 1)*, (ch 3, work Cluster in same sp) twice] across; join with slip st to top of beginning Cluster, finish off: 26 Daisies.

Fig. 1

Rnd 2: With **right** side facing, join MC with slip st in second ch-3 sp; ch 3, 4 dc in same sp, 6 dc in next ch-3 sp, 5 dc in each of next 2 ch-3 sps, 3 dc in each of next 48 ch-3 sps, 5 dc in each of next 2 ch-3 sps, 6 dc in next ch-3 sp, 5 dc in each of next 2 ch-3 sps, 3 dc in each ch-3 sp across to last ch-3 sp, 5 dc in last ch-3 sp; join with slip st to top of beginning ch-3: 340 sts.
Rnd 3: Ch 1, sc in same st, ch 2, skip next dc, (sc in next dc, ch 2, skip next dc) around; join with slip st to first sc: 170 ch-2 sps.
Rnd 4: Slip st in first ch-2 sp, ch 3, 2 dc in same sp, 3 dc in each of next 7 ch-2 sps, 2 dc in each of next 77 ch-2 sps, 3 dc in each of next 8 ch-2 sps, 2 dc in each ch-2 sp across; join with slip st to top of beginning ch-3: 356 sts.
Rnd 5: Repeat Rnd 3; finish off: 178 ch-2 sps.
Rnd 6: With **right** side facing, join Color B with slip st in last ch-2 sp; ch 1, sc in same sp, (ch 3, sc in next ch-2 sp) 89 times, place marker around last ch-3 made for joining placement, ch 3, (sc in next ch-2 sp, ch 3) around; join with slip st to first sc, finish off.

NEXT 4 STRIPS

Work same as First Strip through Rnd 5.

Rnd 6 (Joining rnd)**:** With **right** side facing, join Color B with slip st in last ch-2 sp; ch 1, sc in same sp, (ch 3, sc in next ch-2 sp) 89 times, place marker around last ch-3 made for joining placement, (ch 3, sc in next ch-2 sp) 12 times, ch 2, holding **previous Strip** with **wrong** sides together, sc in marked ch-3 sp on **previous Strip** *(Fig. 24, page 125)*, ch 1, ★ sc in next ch-2 sp on **new Strip**, ch 2, sc in next ch-3 sp on **previous Strip**, ch 1; repeat from ★ across; join with slip st to first sc, finish off.

LAST STRIP

Work same as First Strip through Rnd 5.

Rnd 6 (Joining rnd)**:** With **right** side facing, join Color B with slip st in last ch-2 sp; ch 1, sc in same sp, (ch 3, sc in next ch-2 sp) 101 times, ch 2, holding **previous Strip** with **wrong** sides together, sc in marked ch-3 sp on **previous Strip**, ch 1, ★ sc in next ch-2 sp on **new Strip**, ch 2, sc in next ch-3 sp on **previous Strip**, ch 1; repeat from ★ across; join with slip st to first sc, finish off.

ruffles & ribbons

Mom will love having a frilly afghan for showing off her new baby. This lacy wrap features a simple repeated pattern and can be crocheted in any color to coordinate with the nursery. The flouncy ruffle is trimmed with satin ribbon.

Finished Size: Approximately 30" x 38"

MATERIALS
Baby Yarn, approximately:
  10 ounces, (275 grams, 1,458 yards)
Crochet hook, size G (4.00 mm) **or** size needed
  for gauge
5½ yards of ⅜" wide satin ribbon
Tapestry needle
Sewing needle and thread

GAUGE: (dc, ch 1, dc) 7 times and 9 rows = 4"

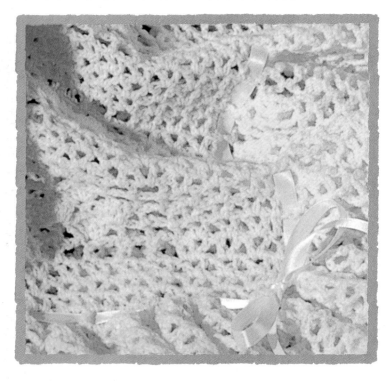

BODY
Ch 128 **loosely**.
Row 1: Dc in eighth ch from hook, (ch 2, skip next 2 chs, dc in next ch) across: 41 sps.
Row 2 (Right side)**:** Ch 5 **(counts as first dc plus ch 2, now and throughout)**, turn; dc in next dc, (dc, ch 1, dc) in next ch-2 sp and in each ch-2 sp across, dc in next dc, ch 2, skip next 2 chs, dc in next ch: 39 ch-1 sps.
Rows 3 and 4: Ch 5, turn; dc in next dc, (dc, ch 1, dc) in next ch-1 sp and in each ch-1 sp across, skip next dc, dc in next dc, ch 2, dc in last dc.
Row 5: Ch 5, turn; dc in next dc, (dc, ch 1, dc) in each of next 3 ch-1 sps, skip next dc, dc in next dc, ★ (ch 2, skip next dc, dc in next dc) 6 times, (dc, ch 1, dc) in each of next 3 ch-1 sps, skip next dc, dc in next dc; repeat from ★ 3 times **more**, ch 2, dc in last dc.
Row 6: Ch 5, turn; dc in next dc, (dc, ch 1, dc) in each of next 3 ch-1 sps, skip next dc, dc in next dc, ★ (ch 2, dc in next dc) twice, 5 dc in next dc, dc in next dc, (ch 2, dc in next dc) twice, (dc, ch 1, dc) in each of next 3 ch-1 sps, skip next dc, dc in next dc; repeat from ★ 3 times **more**, ch 2, dc in last dc.
Row 7: Ch 5, turn; dc in next dc, (dc, ch 1, dc) in each of next 3 ch-1 sps, skip next dc, dc in next dc, ★ ch 2, dc in next dc, 5 dc in next dc, skip next 2 dc, dc in next dc, skip next 2 dc, 5 dc in next dc, dc in next dc, ch 2, dc in next dc, (dc, ch 1, dc) in each of next 3 ch-1 sps, skip next dc, dc in next dc; repeat from ★ 3 times **more**, ch 2, dc in last dc.
Row 8: Ch 5, turn; dc in next dc, (dc, ch 1, dc) in each of next 3 ch-1 sps, skip next dc, dc in next dc, ★ ch 2, dc in next dc, ch 2, skip next 2 dc, dc in next dc, skip next 2 dc, 5 dc in next dc, skip next 2 dc, dc in next dc, ch 2, skip next 2 dc, dc in next dc, ch 2, dc in next dc, (dc, ch 1, dc) in each of next 3 ch-1 sps, skip next dc, dc in next dc; repeat from ★ 3 times **more**, ch 2, dc in last dc.

Row 9: Ch 5, turn; dc in next dc, (dc, ch 1, dc) in each of next 3 ch-1 sps, skip next dc, dc in next dc, ★ (ch 2, dc in next dc) twice, (ch 2, skip next 2 dc, dc in next dc) twice, (ch 2, dc in next dc) twice, (dc, ch 1, dc) in each of next 3 ch-1 sps, skip next dc, dc in next dc; repeat from ★ 3 times **more**, ch 2, dc in last dc.

Row 10: Ch 5, turn; dc in next dc, (dc, ch 1, dc) in each of next 3 ch-1 sps, ★ (dc, ch 1, dc) in each of next 6 ch-2 sps, (dc, ch 1, dc) in each of next 3 ch-1 sps; repeat from ★ 3 times **more**, skip next dc, dc in next dc, ch 2, dc in last dc.

Rows 11 and 12: Ch 5, turn; dc in next dc, (dc, ch 1, dc) in next ch-1 sp and in each ch-1 sp across, skip next dc, dc in next dc, ch 2, dc in last dc.

Rows 13-68: Repeat Rows 5-12, 7 times.

Row 69: Ch 5, turn; dc in next dc, ch 2, skip next 2 dc, dc in next dc, (ch 2, skip next dc, dc in next dc) across to last ch-2 sp, ch 2, dc in last dc; do **not** finish off: 41 ch-2 sps.

RUFFLE

Rnd 1: Ch 1, turn; (sc, ch 5) twice in first sp, (sc, ch 5) 3 times in next sp, [(sc, ch 5) twice in next sp, (sc, ch 5) 3 times in next sp] across to next corner sp, (sc, ch 5) 3 times in corner sp; working in ends of rows, (sc, ch 5) 3 times in next sp, [sc in next sp, ch 5, (sc, ch 5) 3 times in next sp] across to next corner sp, (sc, ch 5) 3 times in corner sp; working over beginning ch, (sc, ch 5) 3 times in next sp, [(sc, ch 5) twice in next sp, (sc, ch 5) 3 times in next sp] across to next corner sp, (sc, ch 5) 3 times in corner sp; working in ends of rows, (sc, ch 5) 3 times in next sp, [sc in next sp, ch 5, (sc, ch 5) 3 times in next sp] across to next corner sp, sc in corner sp, ch 2, dc in first sc to form last sp.

Rnds 2-9: Ch 1, sc in same sp, (ch 5, sc in next ch-5 sp) around, ch 2, dc in first sc to form last sp.

Rnd 10: Ch 1, sc in same sp, ch 5, sc in third ch from hook, ch 2, ★ sc in next ch-5 sp, ch 5, sc in third ch from hook, ch 2; repeat from ★ around; join with slip st to first sc, finish off.

FINISHING

With **right** side facing and leaving 10" ends, refer to photo to weave ribbon through sps at each side of Afghan; tie ribbon ends at each corner in a bow. Use sewing needle and thread to tack bows to Afghan to secure. Trim as desired.

The pretty three-dimensional blooms on this colorful throw bring to mind a field of summer flowers. Green borders around each square enhance the afghan's warm-weather appeal.

Finished Size: Approximately 36" x 49"

MATERIALS

Sport Weight Yarn, approximately:
MC (White) - $13\frac{1}{2}$ ounces, (380 grams, 1,275 yards)
Color A (Green) - 6 ounces, (170 grams, 565 yards)
Color B (Pink) - $\frac{1}{2}$ ounce, (20 grams, 45 yards)
Color C (Peach) - $\frac{1}{2}$ ounce, (20 grams, 45 yards)
Color D (Lavender) - $\frac{1}{2}$ ounce, (20 grams, 45 yards)
Color E (Blue) - $\frac{1}{2}$ ounce, (20 grams, 45 yards)
Color F (Yellow) - $\frac{1}{2}$ ounce, (20 grams, 45 yards)
Crochet hook, size G (4.00 mm) **or** size needed for gauge
Yarn needle

GAUGE: Each Square = $6\frac{3}{4}$"

SQUARE (Make 35)
FLOWER

With Color A, ch 4; join with slip st to form a ring.
Center (Right side)**:** Ch 3 **(counts as first dc, now and throughout)**, 2 dc in ring, ch 2, (3 dc in ring, ch 2) 3 times; join with slip st to first dc, finish off: 12 dc.
Note: Loop a short piece of yarn around any stitch to mark last round as **right** side.

To work **beginning Star**, YO, insert hook in sixth ch from hook, YO and pull up a loop, YO and draw through 2 loops on hook, YO, insert hook in same st as joining, YO and pull up a loop, YO and draw through 2 loops on hook, YO, skip next ch-2 sp, insert hook in next dc, YO and pull up a loop, YO and draw through 2 loops on hook, YO and draw through all 4 loops on hook.

To work **Star**, YO, insert hook in top of last Star made *(Fig. 1a)*, YO and pull up a loop, YO and draw through 2 loops on hook, YO, insert hook in same st as last Star made *(Fig. 1b)*, YO and pull up a loop, YO and draw through 2 loops on hook, YO, skip next st or sp, insert hook in next st *(Fig. 1c)*, YO and pull up a loop, YO and draw through 2 loops on hook, YO and draw through all 4 loops on hook *(Fig. 1d)*.

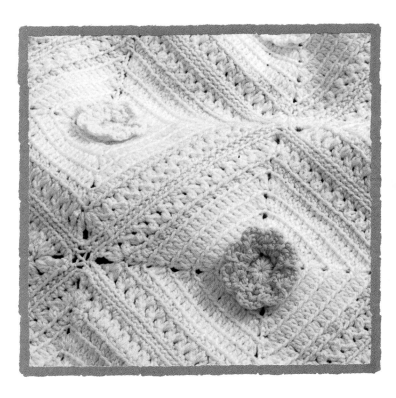

For Petals, make 7 Flowers **each** with Colors B through F.
Petals: With **wrong** side facing and working in Back Loops Only *(Fig. 22, page 125)*, join yarn with slip st in same st as joining; ch 8, work beginning Star, ch 5, (work Star, ch 5) 6 times, YO, insert hook in top of last Star made, YO and pull up a loop, YO and draw through 2 loops on hook, YO, insert hook in same st as last Star made, YO and pull up a loop, YO and draw through 2 loops on hook, skip last dc, insert hook in free loop of third ch of beginning ch-8, YO and draw through ch **and** through all 3 loops on hook; finish off: 8 Petals.

BACKGROUND

Rnd 1: With **right** side facing, working **behind** Petals, and working in free loops and in Back Loops Only of skipped sts on Center *(Fig. 23a, page 125)*, join MC with slip st in second ch of any corner ch-2; ch 3, dc in same st and in next 3 dc, 2 dc in next ch, ★ ch 2, 2 dc in next ch, dc in next 3 dc, 2 dc in next ch; repeat from ★ around, ch 1, sc in first dc to form last ch-2 sp: 28 dc.

Fig. 1a

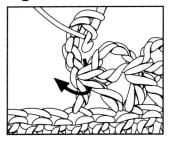

Fig. 1b

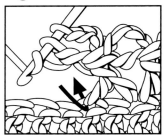

Fig. 1c

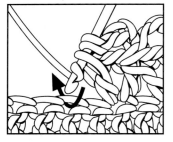

Fig. 1d

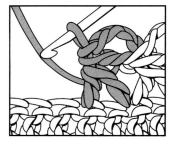

Rnds 2 and 3: Ch 3, dc in side of joining sc, working in Back Loops Only, dc in each dc across to next corner ch-2, 2 dc in next ch, ★ ch 2, 2 dc in next ch, dc in each dc across to next corner ch-2, 2 dc in next ch; repeat from ★ around, ch 1, sc in first dc to form last ch-2 sp: 60 dc.

Rnd 4: Ch 3, dc in side of joining sc, working in Back Loops Only, dc in each dc across to next corner ch-2, 2 dc in next ch, ch 2, ★ 2 dc in next ch, dc in each dc across to next corner ch-2, 2 dc in next ch, ch 2; repeat from ★ around; join with slip st to first dc, finish off: 76 dc.

Rnd 5: With **right** side facing and working in Back Loops Only, join Color A with slip st in first ch of any corner ch-2; ch 2 **(counts as first hdc)**, hdc in same ch, ch 2, 2 hdc in next ch, hdc in each dc across to next corner ch-2, ★ 2 hdc in next ch, ch 2, 2 hdc in next ch, hdc in each dc across to next corner ch-2; repeat from ★ around; join with slip st to first hdc, finish off: 92 hdc.

To work **beginning Cluster**, YO, insert hook in **next** st or sp, YO and pull up a loop, YO and draw through 2 loops on hook, YO, skip next st or sp, insert hook in next st or sp, YO and pull up a loop, YO and draw through 2 loops on hook, YO and draw through all 3 loops on hook.

To work **Cluster**, YO, insert hook in **same** st or sp, YO and pull up a loop, YO and draw through 2 loops on hook, YO, skip next st or sp, insert hook in next st or sp, YO and pull up a loop, YO and draw through 2 loops on hook, YO and draw through all 3 loops on hook.

Rnd 6: With **right** side facing and working in Back Loops Only, join MC with slip st in first ch of any corner ch-2; ch 3, dc in same ch, ch 3, 2 dc in next ch, ch 1, work beginning Cluster, ch 1, (work Cluster, ch 1) across to next corner ch-2, ★ 2 dc in next ch, ch 3, 2 dc in next ch, ch 1, work beginning Cluster, ch 1, (work Cluster, ch 1) across to next corner ch-2; repeat from ★ around; join with slip st to first dc, finish off: 44 Clusters.

Rnd 7: With **right** side facing and working in both loops, join Color A with sc in any corner ch-3 sp **(see Joining with Sc, page 125)**; 2 sc in same sp, sc in each st and in each ch-1 sp across to next corner ch-3 sp, ★ 3 sc in corner ch-3 sp, sc in each st and in each ch-1 sp across to next corner ch-3 sp; repeat from ★ around; join with slip st to first sc, finish off: 120 sc.

ASSEMBLY

With **wrong** sides together and Color A, and working through **inside** loops only, whipstitch Squares together forming 5 vertical strips of 7 Squares each following Placement Diagram **(Fig. 25b, page 126)**; then whipstitch strips together securing seam at each joining.

PLACEMENT DIAGRAM

EDGING

Rnd 1: With **right** side facing and working in Back Loops Only, join MC with sc in first sc to left of any corner 3-sc group; sc in next 27 sc, ★ † sc in same st as joining on **same** Square and in same st as joining on **next** Square, (sc in next 29 sc, sc in same st as joining on **same** Square and in same st as joining on **next** Square) across to last Square on same side of Afghan, sc in next 28 sc, 2 sc in next sc, 3 sc in next sc, 2 sc in next sc †, sc in next 28 sc; repeat from ★ 2 times **more**, then repeat from † to † once; join with slip st to **both** loops of first sc: 756 sc.

Rnd 2: Ch 7, **turn**; working in both loops, YO, insert hook in fifth ch from hook, YO and pull up a loop, YO and draw through 2 loops on hook, YO, insert hook in same st as joining, YO and pull up a loop, YO and draw through 2 loops on hook, YO, skip next sc, insert hook in next sc, YO and pull up a loop, YO and draw through 2 loops on hook, YO and draw through all 4 loops on hook, ch 4, (work Star, ch 4) around to last sc, YO, insert hook in top of last Star made, YO and pull up a loop, YO and draw through 2 loops on hook, YO, insert hook in same st as last Star made, YO and pull up a loop, YO and draw through 2 loops on hook, skip last sc, insert hook in free loop of third ch of beginning ch-7, YO and draw through ch **and** through all 3 loops on hook; finish off.

cheery stripes

Rows of cross stitches and clusters give our cheery wrap a nice textured touch.
Worked from end to end, this rainbow of pastels is a delight to crochet!

Finished Size: Approximately 36" x 45"

MATERIALS
Sport Weight Yarn, approximately:
  Main Color (White) - 15½ ounces,
    (440 grams, 1,465 yards)
  Color A (Blue) - 2 ounces,
    (60 grams, 190 yards)
  Color B (Pink) - 1¾ ounces,
    (50 grams, 165 yards)
  Color C (Green) - 1¾ ounces,
    (50 grams, 165 yards)
  Color D (Yellow) - 1¾ ounces,
    (50 grams, 165 yards)
Crochet hook, size G (4.00 mm) **or** size needed
  for gauge

GAUGE: In pattern, 22 sts and 12 rows = 4"

PATTERN STITCHES
CROSS STITCH
Skip next sc, dc in next sc, ch 1, working **behind**
dc just made, dc in skipped sc *(Fig. 1)*.

Fig. 1

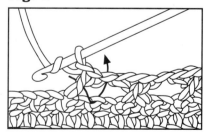

CLUSTER
★ YO, insert hook in Back Loop Only of ch
indicated *(Fig. 22, page 125)*, YO and pull up a
loop, YO and draw through 2 loops on hook;
repeat from ★ 2 times **more**, YO and draw through
all 4 loops on hook *(Figs. 14a & b, page 123)*.
Push Cluster to **right** side.

STRIPE SEQUENCE
2 Rows MC, ★ 1 row Color A, 3 rows MC, 1 row
Color B, 3 rows MC, 1 row Color C, 3 rows MC,
1 row Color D, 3 rows MC; repeat from ★ for
sequence.

Note #1: Each row is worked across length of
Afghan.
Note #2: When joining yarn and finishing off, always
leave a 5" end to be worked into fringe.

BODY
With MC, ch 248.
Row 1: Sc in second ch from hook, (ch 1, skip next
ch, sc in next ch) across: 124 sc.
Row 2 (Right side): Ch 3 **(counts as first hdc plus
ch 1, now and throughout)**, turn; (work Cross St,
ch 1) across to last sc, hdc in last sc; finish off:
61 Cross Sts.
Note: Loop a short piece of yarn around any stitch to
mark last row as **right** side.
Row 3: With **wrong** side facing, join next color with
sc in first hdc *(see Joining with Sc, page 125)*;
ch 1, sc in next dc, work Cluster in next ch, sc in next
dc, ★ (ch 1, sc in next dc) 3 times, work Cluster in
next ch, sc in next dc; repeat from ★ across to last
hdc, ch 1, sc in last hdc; finish off: 31 Clusters.
Row 4: With **right** side facing, join MC with slip st in
first sc; ch 3, (work Cross St, ch 1) across to last sc,
hdc in last sc: 61 Cross Sts.
Row 5: Ch 1, turn; sc in first hdc, ch 1, (sc in next
dc, ch 1) across to last hdc, sc in last hdc: 124 sc.
Row 6: Ch 3, turn; (work Cross St, ch 1) across to
last sc, hdc in last sc; finish off: 61 Cross Sts.
Row 7: With **wrong** side facing, join next color with
sc in first hdc; ★ (ch 1, sc in next dc) 3 times, work
Cluster in next ch, sc in next dc; repeat from ★ across
to last Cross St, ch 1, (sc in next dc, ch 1) twice, sc in
last hdc; finish off: 30 Clusters.
Rows 8 and 9: Repeat Rows 4 and 5.
Repeat Rows 2-9 until Afghan measures approximately
36" from beginning ch, ending by working Row 5; do
not finish off.

EDGING

First Side: Ch 1, turn; slip st in first sc and in next ch-1 sp, (ch 1, skip next sc, slip st in next ch-1 sp) across to last sc, slip st in last sc; finish off.

Second Side: With **right** side facing and working across beginning ch, join MC with slip st in free loop of first ch *(Fig. 23b, page 125)*; slip st in next sp, (ch 1, slip st in next sp) across to last ch, slip st in free loop of last ch; finish off.

FRINGE

Using 3 strands of corresponding color, add fringe across short ends of Afghan *(Figs. 26c & d, page 126)*.

granny's girl

Popcorn stitches add appealing texture to this old-fashioned granny square afghan, which is crocheted with sport weight yarn. With its openwork floral motifs, the captivating coverlet is brimming with feminine style.

Finished Size: Approximately 37" x 46"

MATERIALS
Sport Weight Yarn, approximately:
  25¼ ounces, (720 grams, 2,380 yards)
Crochet hook, size E (3.50 mm) **or** size needed
  for gauge
Yarn needle

GAUGE: Each Square = 4½"

SQUARE (Make 80)
Ch 5; join with slip st to form a ring.
Rnd 1 (Right side): Ch 1, (sc in ring, ch 8) 4 times; join with slip st to first sc: 4 loops.
Note: Loop a short piece of yarn around any stitch to mark last round as **right** side.
Rnd 2: Slip st in first loop, ch 1, work (2 sc, 2 hdc, 2 dc, ch 3, 2 dc, 2 hdc, 2 sc) in same loop and in each loop around; join with slip st to first sc: 48 sts and 4 ch-3 sps.
Rnd 3: Slip st in next 3 sts, ch 4, skip next dc, dc in next dc, (3 dc, ch 3, 3 dc) in next ch-3 sp, dc in next dc, ch 1, skip next dc, dc in next hdc, ch 6, skip next 6 sts, ★ dc in next hdc, ch 1, skip next dc, dc in next dc, (3 dc, ch 3, 3 dc) in next ch-3 sp, dc in next dc, ch 1, skip next dc, dc in next hdc, ch 6, skip next 6 sts; repeat from ★ around; join with slip st to third ch of beginning ch-4: 40 sts and 16 sps.

To work **beginning Popcorn**, ch 3, 4 dc in sp indicated, drop loop from hook, insert hook in top of beginning ch-3, hook dropped loop and draw through.

To work **Popcorn**, work 5 dc in sp indicated, drop loop from hook, insert hook in first dc of 5-dc group, hook dropped loop and draw through *(Fig. 16b, page 123)*.

Rnd 4: Slip st in first ch-1 sp, work beginning Popcorn in same sp, ★ † ch 1, skip next 2 dc, dc in next 2 dc, (3 dc, ch 3, 3 dc) in next ch-3 sp, dc in next 2 dc, ch 1, work Popcorn in next ch-1 sp, ch 2, sc in next loop, ch 2 †, work Popcorn in next ch-1 sp; repeat from ★ 2 times **more**, then repeat from † to † once; join with slip st to top of beginning Popcorn: 52 sts and 20 sps.
Rnd 5: Ch 5, ★ † work Popcorn in next ch-1 sp, ch 2, skip next 2 dc, dc in next 3 dc, (3 dc, ch 3, 3 dc) in next ch-3 sp, dc in next 3 dc, ch 2, work Popcorn in next ch-1 sp, ch 2, dc in next Popcorn, ch 2, dc in next sc, ch 2 †, dc in next Popcorn, ch 2; repeat from ★ 2 times **more**, then repeat from † to † once; join with slip st to third ch of beginning ch-5, finish off: 68 sts and 28 sps.

ASSEMBLY
With **wrong** sides together, and working through **inside** loops only, whipstitch Squares together forming 8 vertical strips of 10 Squares each *(Fig. 25b, page 126)*; then whipstitch Squares together securing seam at each joining.

EDGING
Rnd 1: With **right** side facing and working across short end, join yarn with slip st in top right corner ch-3 sp; ch 1, 2 sc in same sp, † work 189 sc evenly spaced across to next corner ch-3 sp, 3 sc in corner ch-3 sp, work 231 sc evenly spaced across to next corner ch-3 sp †, 3 sc in corner ch-3 sp, repeat from † to † once, sc in same sp as first sc; join with slip st to first sc: 852 sc.
Rnd 2: Ch 3, 4 dc in same st, ch 1, skip next 2 sc, sc in next sc, ch 1, skip next 2 sc, ★ 5 dc in next sc, ch 1, skip next 2 sc, sc in next sc, ch 1, skip next 2 sc; repeat from ★ around; join with slip st to top of beginning ch-3, finish off.

rock·a·bye rainsong

This snuggly afghan will wrap baby in tranquil softness. The shaded stripes bring to mind cascading raindrops in a gentle April shower.

Finished Size: Approximately 38" x 45"

MATERIALS
Worsted Weight Yarn, approximately:
   MC (Blue) - 9 ounces, (260 grams, 525 yards)
   Color A (White) - 10 ounces,
     (280 grams, 585 yards)
   Color B (Light Blue) - 8 ounces,
     (230 grams, 470 yards)
Crochet hook, size I (5.50 mm) **or** size needed for gauge

GAUGE: In pattern, 14 sts and 9 rows = 4"

STRIPE SEQUENCE
Work 2 rows of each color: MC, ★ Color A, Color B, MC; repeat from ★ throughout *(Fig. 21a, page 125)*.

BODY
With MC, ch 125 **loosely**.

Row 1: Dc in fourth ch from hook and in next ch **(3 skipped chs count as first dc)**, (ch 1, skip next ch, dc in next 3 chs) across: 30 ch-1 sps.

Row 2 (Right side)**:** Ch 3 **(counts as first dc, now and throughout)**, turn; dc in next 2 dc, (ch 1, dc in next 3 dc) across.

Note: Loop a short piece of yarn around any stitch to mark last row as **right** side.

To work **Long double crochet (abbreviated Ldc)**, YO, working **around** next ch-1, insert hook in ch-1 sp one row **below** *(Fig. 8, page 122)*, YO and pull up a loop even with last st made, (YO and draw through 2 loops on hook) twice.

Row 3: Ch 4 **(counts as first dc plus ch 1, now and throughout)**, turn; skip next dc, dc in next dc, ★ work Ldc, dc in next dc, ch 1, skip next dc, dc in next dc; repeat from ★ across: 31 ch-1 sps.

Row 4: Ch 4, turn; skip first ch-1 sp, ★ dc in next 3 sts, ch 1, skip next ch-1 sp; repeat from ★ across to last dc, dc in last dc.

Row 5: Ch 3, turn; work Ldc, dc in next dc, ★ ch 1, skip next dc, dc in next dc, work Ldc, dc in next dc; repeat from ★ across: 30 ch-1 sps.

Row 6: Ch 3, turn; dc in next 2 sts, ★ ch 1, skip next ch-1 sp, dc in next 3 sts; repeat from ★ across.

Rows 7-97: Repeat Rows 3-6, 22 times; then repeat Rows 3-5 once **more**.

Row 98: Ch 3, turn; dc in next st and in each st and each ch-1 sp across; finish off.

EDGING
Rnd 1: With **right** side facing, join Color A with slip st in first dc on last row; ch 1, 3 sc in same st, work 119 sc evenly spaced across to last dc, 3 sc in last dc; work 167 sc evenly spaced across end of rows to beginning ch; working in free loops of beginning ch *(Fig. 23b, page 125)*, 3 sc in first ch, work 119 sc evenly spaced across to last ch, 3 sc in last ch; work 167 sc evenly spaced across end of rows; join with slip st to first sc: 584 sc.

Rnd 2: Ch 1, sc in same st and in each sc around, working 3 sc in each corner sc; join with slip st to first sc: 592 sc.

Rnd 3: ★ Ch 2, skip next sc, 3 dc in next sc, ch 2, skip next sc, slip st in next sc, (ch 2, skip next 2 sc, 3 dc in next sc, ch 2, skip next 2 sc, slip st in next sc) across to within one sc of corner; repeat from ★ 2 times **more**, ch 2, skip next sc, 3 dc in next sc, ch 2, skip next sc, (slip st in next sc, ch 2, skip next 2 sc, 3 dc in next sc, ch 2, skip next 2 sc) across; join with slip st in same st as joining, finish off.

Lacy ripples of soft green, pink, and white form this cuddly cover-up.
For dainty flair, a white picot edging embellishes the throw.

Finished Size: Approximately 35" x 44"

MATERIALS
Sport Weight Yarn, approximately:
  MC (Green) - 6 ounces,
    (170 grams, 565 yards)
  Color A (White) - 5¼ ounces,
    (150 grams, 495 yards)
  Color B (Pink) - 5¼ ounces,
    (150 grams, 495 yards)
  Crochet hook, size F (3.75 mm) **or** size needed
    for gauge

GAUGE: In pattern, 19 sts (point to point) = 2½"
    and 7 rows = 4

STRIPE SEQUENCE
One row **each** color: MC, ★ Color B, Color A, MC;
repeat from ★ 24 times **more (Fig. 21a, page 125)**.

BODY
Ch 229 **loosely**.
Row 1 (Right side)**:** Dc in sixth ch from hook, ch 1,
skip next ch, (dc in next ch, ch 1, skip next ch) twice,
(dc, ch 1) 4 times in next ch, skip next ch, dc in next
ch, (ch 1, skip next ch, dc in next ch) twice, ★ skip
next 3 chs, (dc in next ch, ch 1, skip next ch) 3 times,
(dc, ch 1) 4 times in next ch, skip next ch, dc in next
ch, (ch 1, skip next ch, dc in next ch) twice; repeat
from ★ across to last 3 chs, skip next 2 chs, dc in last
ch: 141 dc and 126 ch-1 sps.
Note: Loop a short piece of yarn around any stitch to
mark last row as **right** side.
Row 2: Ch 3 **(counts as first dc, now and**
throughout), turn; skip first ch-1 sp, dc in next
ch-1 sp, (ch 1, dc in next ch-1 sp) twice, (ch 1, dc) 4
times in next ch-1 sp, (ch 1, dc in next ch-1 sp) 3
times, ★ skip next 2 ch-1 sps, dc in next ch-1 sp,
(ch 1, dc in next ch-1 sp) twice, (ch 1, dc) 4 times in
next ch-1 sp, (ch 1, dc in next ch-1 sp) 3 times; repeat
from ★ across to last 2 dc, skip last 2 dc, dc in top of
beginning ch: 142 dc and 126 ch-1 sps.

Rows 3-76: Ch 3, turn; skip first ch-1 sp, dc in next
ch-1 sp, (ch 1, dc in next ch-1 sp) twice, (ch 1, dc) 4
times in next ch-1 sp, (ch 1, dc in next ch-1 sp) 3
times, ★ skip next 2 ch-1 sps, dc in next ch-1 sp,
(ch 1, dc in next ch-1 sp) twice, (ch 1, dc) 4 times in
next ch-1 sp, (ch 1, dc in next ch-1 sp) 3 times; repeat
from ★ across to last 3 dc, skip next 2 dc, dc in last
dc.
Finish off.

EDGING
To work **Picot**, ch 3, sc in third ch from hook.
With **right** side facing, join Color A with sc in first
ch-1 sp on Row 76 **(see Joining with Sc, page**
125); **[**(work Picot, sc in next ch-1 sp) 8 times, skip
next 2 dc, sc in next ch-1 sp**]** 13 times, work Picot, (sc
in next ch-1 sp, work Picot) 8 times; working in end of
rows, (sc, work Picot, sc) in each row across to last
row, (sc, work Picot) 3 times in last row; working over
beginning ch, (sc, work Picot) in next 2 ch-1 sps, sc in
next 2 ch-1 sps, work Picot, (sc in next ch-1 sp, work
Picot) twice, ★ (sc, work Picot) twice in next ch-3 sp,
(sc in next ch-1 sp, work Picot) twice, sc in next
2 ch-1 sps, work Picot, (sc in next ch-1 sp, work Picot)
twice; repeat from ★ 12 times **more**, sc in next sp,
(work Picot, sc in same sp) twice; working in end of
rows, (sc, work Picot, sc) in next row and in each row
across to last row, (sc, work Picot) twice in last row;
join with slip st to first sc, finish off.

hugs & kisses

Featuring floral motifs that create a pattern of X's and O's, this afghan will wrap your little one in hugs and kisses. The petals are worked first and then the background of each square is completed, creating a three-dimensional look.

Finished Size: Approximately 35" x 49"

MATERIALS

Sport Weight Yarn, approximately:
MC (White) - 13 ounces,
   (370 grams, 1,225 yards)
Color A (Yellow) - 3½ ounces,
   (100 grams, 330 yards)
Color B (Blue) - 4 ounces,
   (110 grams, 375 yards)
Color C (Green) - 3½ ounces,
   (100 grams, 330 yards)
Crochet hook, size G (4.00 mm) **or** size needed
   for gauge
Yarn needle

GAUGE: Each Square = 6¾"

SQUARE X (Make 18)
CENTER

With Color A, ch 4; join with slip st to form a ring.

Rnd 1 (Right side)**:** Ch 3 **(counts as first dc, now and throughout)**, 2 dc in ring, ch 2, (3 dc in ring, ch 2) 3 times; join with slip st to first dc, finish off: 12 dc.

Note: Loop a short piece of yarn around any stitch to mark last round as **right** side.

Rnd 2: With **right** side facing and working in Front Loops Only *(Fig. 22, page 125)*, join Color B with sc in second ch of any corner ch-2 *(see Joining with Sc, page 125)*; sc in next 3 dc and in next ch, ch 11, ★ sc in next ch, sc in next 3 dc and in next ch, ch 11; repeat from ★ around; join with slip st to **both** loops of first sc: 4 loops.

Rnd 3: Working in both loops, slip st in next 2 sc, ch 1, sc in same st, 9 dc in next loop, place marker around last dc made for joining placement, 9 dc in same loop, ★ skip next 2 sc, sc in next sc, 9 dc in next loop, place marker around last dc made for joining placement, 9 dc in same loop; repeat from ★ around; join with slip st to first sc: 72 dc.

Rnd 4: ★ **[**(Sc, ch 3, sc) in next dc, skip next dc**]** 4 times, (sc, ch 3, sc) in Front Loop Only of next dc, skip next dc, **[**(sc, ch 3, sc) in **both** loops of next dc, skip next dc**]** 4 times, slip st in next sc; repeat from ★ around working last slip st in same st as joining; finish off: 36 ch-3 sps.

BACKGROUND

Rnd 1: With **right** side facing, working **behind** previous rnds, and working in free loops on Rnd 1 of Center *(Fig. 23a, page 125)*, join MC with slip st in second ch of any corner ch-2; ch 3, dc in same st and in next 3 dc, 2 dc in next ch, ★ ch 2, 2 dc in next ch, dc in next 3 dc, 2 dc in next ch; repeat from ★ around, ch 1, sc in first dc to form last ch-2 sp: 28 dc.

Rnds 2 and 3: Ch 3, dc in side of joining sc, working in Back Loops Only, dc in each dc across to next corner ch-2, 2 dc in next ch, ★ ch 2, 2 dc in next ch, dc in each dc across to next corner ch-2, 2 dc in next ch; repeat from ★ around, ch 1, sc in first dc to form last ch-2 sp: 60 dc.

Rnd 4: Ch 3, dc in side of joining sc, working in Back Loops Only, dc in each dc across to next corner ch-2, 2 dc in next ch, ch 1, slip st in free loop of marked dc on Rnd 3 of Center, ch 1, ★ 2 dc in next ch, dc in each dc across to next corner ch-2, 2 dc in next ch, ch 1, slip st in free loop of marked dc on Rnd 3 of Center, ch 1; repeat from ★ around; join with slip st to first dc, finish off: 76 dc.

Rnd 5: With **right** side facing and working in Back Loops Only, join Color C with slip st in first ch of any corner; ch 2 **(counts as first hdc, now and throughout)**, hdc in same ch, ch 2, skip next slip st, 2 hdc in next ch, hdc in each dc across to next corner, ★ 2 hdc in next ch, ch 2, skip next slip st, 2 hdc in next ch, hdc in each dc across to next corner; repeat from ★ around; join with slip st to first hdc, finish off: 92 hdc.

To work **beginning Cluster**, YO, insert hook in **next** st or sp, YO and pull up a loop, YO and draw through 2 loops on hook, YO, skip next st or sp, insert hook in next st or sp, YO and pull up a loop, YO and draw through 2 loops on hook, YO and draw through all 3 loops on hook.

To work **Cluster**, YO, insert hook in **same** st or sp, YO and pull up a loop, YO and draw through 2 loops on hook, YO, skip next st or sp, insert hook in next st or sp, YO and pull up a loop, YO and draw through 2 loops on hook, YO and draw through all 3 loops on hook.

Rnd 6: With **right** side facing and working in Back Loops Only, join MC with slip st in first ch of any corner ch-2; ch 3, dc in same ch, ch 3, 2 dc in next ch, ch 1, work beginning Cluster, ch 1, (work Cluster, ch 1) across to next corner ch-2, ★ 2 dc in next ch, ch 3, 2 dc in next ch, ch 1, work beginning Cluster, ch 1, (work Cluster, ch 1) across to next corner ch-2; repeat from ★ around; join with slip st to first dc, finish off: 44 Clusters.

Rnd 7: With **right** side facing and working in both loops, join Color A with sc in any corner ch-3 sp; 2 sc in same sp, sc in each st and in each ch-1 sp across to next corner ch-3 sp, ★ 3 sc in corner ch-3 sp, sc in each st and in each ch-1 sp across to next corner ch-3 sp; repeat from ★ around; join with slip st to first sc, finish off: 120 sc.

SQUARE O (Make 17)
FLOWER

With Color A, ch 4; join with slip st to form a ring.
Center (Right side)**:** Ch 3, 2 dc in ring, ch 2, (3 dc in ring, ch 2) 3 times; join with slip st to first dc, finish off: 12 dc.
Note: Mark last round as **right** side.

To work **beginning Star**, YO, insert hook in sixth ch from hook, YO and pull up a loop, YO and draw through 2 loops on hook, YO, insert hook in same st as joining, YO and pull up a loop, YO and draw through 2 loops on hook, YO, skip next ch-2 sp, insert hook in next dc, YO and pull up a loop, YO and draw through 2 loops on hook, YO and draw through all 4 loops on hook.

To work **Star**, YO, insert hook in top of last Star made *(Fig. 1a)*, YO and pull up a loop, YO and draw through 2 loops on hook, YO, insert hook in same st as last Star made *(Fig. 1b)*, YO and pull up a loop, YO and draw through 2 loops on hook, YO, skip next st or sp, insert hook in next st *(Fig. 1c)*, YO and pull up a loop, YO and draw through 2 loops on hook, YO and draw through all 4 loops on hook *(Fig. 1d)*.

Fig. 1a

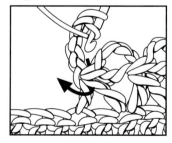

Fig. 1b

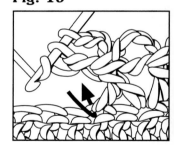

Fig. 1c

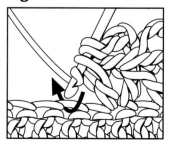

Fig. 1d

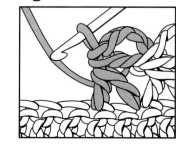

Petals: With **wrong** side facing and working in Back Loops Only, join Color B with slip st in same st as joining; ch 8, work beginning Star, ch 5, (work Star, ch 5) 6 times, YO, insert hook in top of last Star made, YO and pull up a loop, YO and draw through 2 loops on hook, YO, insert hook in same st as last Star made, YO and pull up a loop, YO and draw through 2 loops on hook, skip last dc, insert hook in free loop of third ch of beginning ch-8, YO and draw through ch **and** through all 3 loops on hook; finish off: 8 Petals.

BACKGROUND
Rnd 1: With **right** side facing, working **behind** Petals, and working in free loops and in Back Loops Only of skipped sts on Center, join MC with slip st in second ch of any corner ch-2; ch 3, dc in same st and in next 3 dc, 2 dc in next ch, ★ ch 2, 2 dc in next ch, dc in next 3 dc, 2 dc in next ch; repeat from ★ around, ch 1, sc in first dc to form last ch-2 sp: 28 dc.
Rnds 2 and 3: Ch 3, dc in side of joining sc, working in Back Loops Only, dc in each dc across to next corner ch-2, 2 dc in next ch, ★ ch 2, 2 dc in next ch, dc in each dc across to next corner ch-2, 2 dc in next ch; repeat from ★ around, ch 1, sc in first dc to form last ch-2 sp: 60 dc.
Rnd 4: Ch 3, dc in side of joining sc, working in Back Loops Only, dc in each dc across to next corner ch-2, 2 dc in next ch, ch 2, ★ 2 dc in next ch, dc in each dc across to next corner ch-2, 2 dc in next ch, ch 2; repeat from ★ around; join with slip st to first dc, finish off: 76 dc.
Rnd 5: With **right** side facing and working in Back Loops Only, join Color C with slip st in first ch of any corner ch-2; ch 2, hdc in same ch, ch 2, 2 hdc in next ch, hdc in each dc across to next corner ch-2, ★ 2 hdc in next ch, ch 2, 2 hdc in next ch, hdc in each dc across to next corner ch-2; repeat from ★ around; join with slip st to first hdc, finish off: 92 hdc.
Rnd 6: With **right** side facing and working in Back Loops Only, join MC with slip st in first ch of any corner ch-2; ch 3, dc in same ch, ch 3, 2 dc in next ch, ch 1, work beginning Cluster, ch 1, (work Cluster, ch 1) across to next corner ch-2, ★ 2 dc in next ch, ch 3, 2 dc in next ch, ch 1, work beginning Cluster, ch 1, (work Cluster, ch 1) across to next corner ch-2; repeat from ★ around; join with slip st to first dc, finish off: 44 Clusters.
Rnd 7: With **right** side facing and working in both loops, join Color A with sc in any corner ch-3 sp; 2 sc in same sp, sc in each st and in each ch-1 sp across to next corner ch-3 sp, ★ 3 sc in corner ch-3 sp, sc in each st and in each ch-1 sp across to next corner ch-3 sp; repeat from ★ around; join with slip st to first sc, finish off: 120 sc.

ASSEMBLY
With **wrong** sides together and Color A, and working through **inside** loops only, whipstitch Squares together forming 5 vertical strips of 7 Squares each following Placement Diagram *(Fig. 25b, page 126)*; then whipstitch strips together securing seam at each joining.

PLACEMENT DIAGRAM

X	O	X	O	X
O	X	O	X	O
X	O	X	O	X
O	X	O	X	O
X	O	X	O	X
O	X	O	X	O
X	O	X	O	X

EDGING
Rnd 1: With **right** side facing and working in Back Loops Only, join MC with sc in center sc of any corner; sc in same st, ★ † sc in next 29 sc, (sc in same st as joining on **same** Square and in same st as joining on **next** Square, sc in next 29 sc) across to center sc of next corner †, 2 sc in center sc; repeat from ★ 2 times **more**, then repeat from † to † once; join with slip st to **both** loops of first sc: 744 sc.
Rnd 2: Ch 3, working in both loops, dc in same st, ch 2, 2 dc in next sc, dc in each sc across to next corner 2-sc group, ★ 2 dc in next sc, ch 2, 2 dc in next sc, dc in each sc across to next corner 2-sc group; repeat from ★ around; join with slip st to first dc, finish off: 752 dc.
Rnd 3: With **right** side facing, join Color C with slip st in any dc; ch 1, working from **left** to **right**, work reverse sc in each dc and in each ch around *(Figs. 18a-d, page 124)*; join with slip st to first st, finish off.

sweet softness

*Baby's face will light up with smiles when she touches this soft cover-up!
The simple motifs, worked in pink and white worsted weight yarn, bring to
mind images of fluffy cotton candy. Pink fringe adds a pretty touch.*

Finished Size: Approximately 38" x 45"

MATERIALS
Worsted Weight Yarn, approximately:
  MC (Pink) - 10 ounces, (280 grams, 660 yards)
  CC (White) - 15 ounces, (430 grams, 985 yards)
Crochet hook, size I (5.50 mm) **or** size needed
  for gauge
Yarn needle

GAUGE: Each Square = 7¹/₂"

SQUARE (Make 30)
Rnd 1 (Right side)**:** With MC, ch 4, 2 dc in fourth ch
from hook, ch 2, (3 dc, ch 2) 3 times in same ch; join
with slip st to top of beginning ch-4: 4 ch-2 sps.
Note: Loop a short piece of yarn around any stitch to
mark last round as **right** side.
Rnd 2: Ch 4, skip next dc, dc in next dc, ch 1, (dc,
ch 2, dc) in next ch-2 sp, ch 1, ★ dc in next dc, ch 1,
skip next dc, dc in next dc, ch 1, (dc, ch 2, dc) in next
ch-2 sp, ch 1; repeat from ★ around; join with slip st
to third ch of beginning ch-4: 16 sps.
Rnd 3: Ch 4, dc in next dc, ch 1, dc in next dc,
(2 dc, ch 1, 2 dc) in next ch-2 sp, dc in next dc,
★ (ch 1, dc in next dc) 3 times, (2 dc, ch 1, 2 dc) in
next ch-2 sp, dc in next dc; repeat from ★ 2 times
more, ch 1; join with slip st to third ch of beginning
ch-4, finish off.
Rnd 4: With **right** side facing, join CC with sc in any
corner ch-1 sp *(see Joining with Sc, page 125)*,
ch 2, sc in same sp, ★ sc in each dc and in each ch-1
sp across to next corner ch-1 sp, (sc, ch 2, sc) in ch-1
sp; repeat from ★ 2 times **more**, sc in each dc and in
each ch-1 sp across; join with slip st to first sc: 52 sc.

Rnd 5: Slip st in first ch-2 sp, ch 1, 3 sc in same sp,
skip next sc, sc in next 11 sc, skip next sc, ★ 3 sc in
next ch-2 sp, skip next sc, sc in next 11 sc, skip next
sc; repeat from ★ around; join with slip st to first sc,
finish off.
Rnd 6: With **wrong** side facing, join MC with sc in
same st as joining; ★ † (pull up a loop in same st and
in next st, YO and draw through all 3 loops on hook)
12 times, ch 1, dc in next sc, ch 1 †, sc in next sc;
repeat from ★ 2 times **more**, then repeat from † to †
once; join with slip st to first sc, finish off.
Rnd 7: With **right** side facing, join CC with slip st in
any corner dc; ch 3, (dc, ch 1, 2 dc) in same dc,
★ † skip next ch, 2 dc in next st, (skip next st, 2 dc in
next st) 6 times, skip next ch †, (2 dc, ch 1, 2 dc) in
next corner dc; repeat from ★ 2 times **more**, then
repeat from † to † once; join with slip st to top of
beginning ch-3.
Rnd 8: Slip st in next dc and in next ch-1 sp, ch 3,
(dc, ch 1, 2 dc) in same sp, 2 dc in sp **between** each
2-dc group across to next corner ch-1 sp, ★ (2 dc,
ch 1, 2 dc) in ch-1 sp, 2 dc in sp **between** each 2-dc
group across to next corner ch-1 sp; repeat from ★
around; join with slip st to top of beginning ch-3,
finish off: 80 sts.

ASSEMBLY
With **wrong** sides together and CC, and working
through **inside** loops only, whipstitch Squares together
forming 5 vertical strips of 6 Squares each *(Fig. 25b,
page 126)*; then whipstitch strips together.

FRINGE
Using 3, 9" strands of MC, add fringe in every other
stitch across each end of Afghan *(Figs. 26a & b,
page 126)*.

rolling ripples

Gentle rolling waves of mint green make this afghan a good choice for boys or girls. Treble crochet stitches and chain spaces form the lacy openwork between solid ripples of half double crochets.

Finished Size: Approximately 38½" x 52"

MATERIALS
Sport Weight Yarn, approximately:
   20 ounces, (570 grams, 2,000 yards)
   Crochet hook, size H (5.00 mm) **or** size needed
   for gauge

GAUGE: 16 hdc and 12 rows = 4"

BODY
Ch 155 **loosely**.
Row 1 (Right side)**:** Hdc in third ch from hook and in each ch across: 154 sts.
Note: Loop a short piece of yarn around any stitch to mark last row as **right** side.
To work **hdc decrease**, YO, insert hook in next hdc, YO and pull up a loop, YO, skip next hdc, insert hook in next hdc, YO and pull up a loop, YO and draw through all 5 loops on hook **(Fig. 1, counts as one hdc)**.

Fig. 1

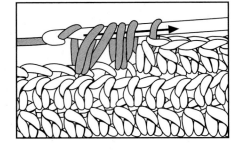

Row 2: Ch 2 **(counts as first hdc, now and throughout)**, turn; hdc in next 8 hdc, hdc decrease, ★ hdc in next 7 hdc, 2 hdc in each of next 2 hdc, hdc in next 7 hdc, hdc decrease; repeat from ★ across to last 9 hdc, hdc in last 9 hdc: 152 hdc.

Row 3: Ch 2, turn; hdc in next hdc and in each hdc across.
To work **tr decrease**, YO twice, insert hook in next hdc, YO and pull up a loop, (YO and draw through 2 loops on hook) twice, YO twice, skip next hdc, insert hook in next hdc, YO and pull up a loop, (YO and draw through 2 loops on hook) twice, YO and draw through all 3 loops on hook **(Fig. 2, counts as one tr)**.

Fig. 2

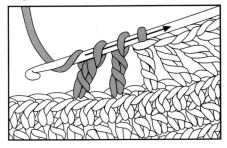

Row 4: Ch 5 **(counts as first tr plus ch 1)**, turn; (tr, ch 1) twice in same st, ★ † (skip next hdc, tr in next hdc) 3 times, skip next hdc, tr decrease, (skip next hdc, tr in next hdc) 3 times, skip next hdc, (ch 1, tr) 3 times in next hdc †, (tr, ch 1) 3 times in next hdc; repeat from ★ 6 times **more**, then repeat from † to † once: 104 tr.
Row 5: Ch 2, turn; hdc in same tr and in each ch and tr across to last tr, 2 hdc in last tr: 154 hdc.
Repeat Rows 2-5 until Afghan measures approximately 52" from beginning ch, ending by working Row 3. Finish off.

easter mile·a·minute

Worked in strips of springtime green, lavender, and yellow, this afghan calls up images of colorful dyed eggs. It'll be a great Easter blanket for baby!

Finished Size: Approximately 39" x 48"

MATERIALS
Sport Weight Yarn, approximately:
   Color A (Green) - 6 ounces,
      (170 grams, 565 yards)
   Color B (Lavender) - 7½ ounces,
      (210 grams, 710 yards)
   Color C (Yellow) - 3½ ounces,
      (100 grams, 330 yards)
   Crochet hook, size H (5.00 mm) **or** size needed
      for gauge

GAUGE: 16 dc and 8 rows = 4"
      Each Strip = 4¼" wide

FIRST STRIP
With Color A, ch 166 **loosely**.
Rnd 1 (Right side)**:** Dc in fourth ch from hook **(3 skipped chs count as first dc)**, ch 1, (dc in same ch, ch 1) twice, 2 dc in same ch, [skip next 2 chs, (dc, ch 1, dc) in next ch] across to last 3 chs, skip next 2 chs, in last ch work [2 dc, ch 1, (dc, ch 1) twice, 2 dc]; working in free loops of beginning ch *(Fig. 23b, page 125)*, skip next 2 chs, ★ (dc, ch 1, dc) in next ch, skip next 2 chs; repeat from ★ across; join with slip st to first dc: 224 dc and 112 ch-1 sps.
Note: Loop a short piece of yarn around any stitch to mark last round as **right** side.
Rnd 2: Ch 1, sc in same st and in each dc and each ch-1 sp around; join with slip st to first sc, finish off: 336 sc.
Rnd 3: With **right** side facing and working in Back Loops Only *(Fig. 22, page 125)*, join Color B with slip st in center sc on either end; ch 3 **(counts as first dc)**, dc in same st, ch 1, dc in next 3 sc, ch 1, 3 dc in next sc, ch 1, (dc in next 3 sc, ch 1) 53 times, 3 dc in next sc, ch 1, (dc in next 3 sc, ch 1, 3 dc in next sc, ch 1) twice, (dc in next 3 sc, ch 1) across to last 4 sc, 3 dc in next sc, ch 1, dc in last 3 sc, ch 1, dc in same st as first dc; join with slip st to first dc: 348 dc and 116 ch-1 sps.

Rnd 4: Ch 2, working in both loops, 2 hdc in same st, slip st in next ch-1 sp, skip next dc, (3 hdc in next dc, slip st in next ch-1 sp, skip next dc) around; join with slip st to top of beginning ch-2, finish off: 464 sts.
Rnd 5: With **right** side facing and working in Back Loops Only, join Color C with sc in second slip st to **right** of joining *(see Joining with Sc, page 125)*; (2 sc, ch 1, 3 sc) in same st, † ★ ch 4, slip st in last sc made, skip next 3 sts, (3 sc, ch 1, 3 sc) in next slip st; repeat from ★ 2 times **more**, ch 1, (skip next 3 hdc, 3 hdc in next slip st, ch 1) 54 times, skip next 3 hdc †, (3 sc, ch 1, 3 sc) in next slip st, repeat from † to † once; join with slip st to **both** loops of first sc, finish off.

REMAINING 8 STRIPS
Work same as First Strip through Rnd 4: 464 sts.
Rnd 5 (Joining rnd)**:** With **right** side facing and working in Back Loops Only, join Color C with sc in second slip st to **right** of joining; (2 sc, ch 1, 3 sc) in same st, † [ch 4, slip st in last sc made, skip next 3 sts, (3 sc, ch 1, 3 sc) in next slip st] 3 times, ch 1 †, (skip next 3 hdc, 3 hdc in next slip st, ch 1) 54 times, skip next 3 hdc, (3 sc, ch 1, 3 sc) in next slip st, repeat from † to † once, skip next 3 hdc, 3 hdc in next slip st, ch 1, holding Strips with **wrong** sides together, ★ slip st in corresponding ch-1 sp on **previous Strip** *(Fig. 24, page 125)*, ch 1, skip next 3 hdc on **new Strip**, 3 hdc in next slip st, ch 1; repeat from ★ across; join with slip st to **both** loops of first sc, finish off.

hearts and bows

Your little princess will look precious in this sweetheart of an afghan, which features filet crochet hearts. White satin ribbon is woven through the eyelet round in the ruffled border and tied into bows to complete the romantic look.

Finished Size: Approximately 41" x 50"

MATERIALS
Sport Weight Yarn, approximately:
20 ounces, (570 grams, 1,885 yards)
Crochet hook, size F (3.75 mm) **or** size needed for gauge
7 yards of ⅜" wide ribbon
Yarn needle

GAUGE: 18 dc and 9 rows = 4"

BASIC CHART STITCHES
Space over Space: Ch 2, dc in next dc.
Block over Block: Dc in next 3 dc.
Beginning Block over Block: Ch 3, turn; dc in next 3 dc.
Block over Space: 2 Dc in next ch-2 sp, dc in next dc.
Space over Block: Ch 2, skip next 2 dc, dc in next dc.

BODY
Ch 168 **loosely**.
Row 1 (Right side): Dc in fourth ch from hook and in next 2 chs **(3 skipped chs count as first dc)**, ch 2, skip next 2 chs, dc in next ch, ch 2, skip next 2 chs, dc in next 4 chs, ★ ch 2, skip next 2 chs, (dc in next ch, ch 2, skip next 2 chs) 12 times, dc in next 4 chs, ch 2, skip next 2 chs, dc in next ch, ch 2, skip next 2 chs, dc in next 4 chs; repeat from ★ across: 47 ch-2 sps.
Note: Loop a short piece of yarn around any stitch to mark last row as **right** side.
Row 2: Ch 3 **(counts as first dc, now and throughout)**, turn; dc in next 3 dc, ch 2, slip st in next dc, work Space over Space, work Block over Block, ★ work Space over Space 13 times, work Block over Block, ch 2, slip st in next dc, work Space over Space, work Block over Block; repeat from ★ across.

Row 3: Work Beginning Block over Block, ch 2, tr in next slip st, work Space over Space, work Block over Block, ★ work Space over Space 13 times, work Block over Block, ch 2, tr in next slip st, work Space over Space, work Block over Block; repeat from ★ across.
Row 4: Work Beginning Block over Block, ch 2, slip st in next tr, work Space over Space, work Block over Block, ★ work Space over Space 6 times, work Block over Space, work Space over Space 6 times, work Block over Block, ch 2, slip st in next tr, work Space over Space, work Block over Block; repeat from ★ across.
Rows 5-17: Follow Chart.
Rows 18-101: Repeat Rows 4-17, 6 times.
Row 102: Work Beginning Block over Block, ch 2, dc in next tr, work Space over Space, work Block over Block, ★ work Space over Space 13 times, work Block over Block, ch 2, dc in next tr, work Space over Space, work Block over Block; repeat from ★ across; do **not** finish off.

CHART

- Row 17
- Row 4
- Row 1

repeat

KEY
☐ - Space
▨ - Block

EDGING

Rnd 1 (Eyelet rnd)**:** Ch 6, turn; working in chs and in dc across last row, dc in same st (corner), ch 1, dc in next dc, ch 1, (skip next st, dc in next st, ch 1) across to last 2 dc, dc in next dc, ch 1, (dc, ch 3, dc) in last dc (corner), ch 1; working across end of rows, (dc in top of dc on next row, ch 1) across; working in free loops of beginning ch *(Fig. 23b, page 125)*, (dc, ch 3, dc) in first ch (corner), ch 1, dc in next ch, ch 1, (skip next ch, dc in next ch, ch 1) across to last 2 chs, dc in next ch, ch 1, (dc, ch 3, dc) in last ch (corner), ch 1; working across end of rows, (dc in top of dc on next row, ch 1) across; join with slip st to third ch of beginning ch-6: 372 ch-1 sps.

Rnd 2: Ch 5 **(counts as first dc plus ch 2, now and throughout)**, dc in same st, ch 2, (dc, ch 2) 4 times in next corner ch-3 sp, ★ (dc, ch 2) twice in next dc, **[**dc in next dc, ch 2, (dc, ch 2) twice in next dc**]** across to next corner ch-3 sp, (dc, ch 2) 4 times in corner ch-3 sp; repeat from ★ 2 times **more, [**(dc, ch 2) twice in next dc, dc in next dc, ch 2**]** across; join with slip st to first dc.

Rnd 3: Slip st in first ch-2 sp, ch 5, (dc in next ch-2 sp, ch 2) around; join with slip st to first dc.
Rnd 4: Ch 5, (dc in next dc, ch 2) around; join with slip st to first dc.
Rnd 5: Slip st in first ch-2 sp, ch 3, (slip st in next ch-2 sp, ch 3) around; join with slip st to first slip st, finish off.

FINISHING

Weave ribbon through Eyelet rnd along each side of Afghan, leaving 10" ends. Tie ends in a bow at each corner.

simply beautiful

Simply beautiful, this blanket of shells will soothe baby to sleep. The cozy cover-up is quick to crochet using variegated sport weight yarn.

Finished Size: Approximately 34" x 46"

MATERIALS
Sport Weight Yarn, approximately:
    18 ounces, (510 grams, 1,935 yards)
Crochet hook, size F (3.75 mm) **or** size needed
    for gauge

GAUGE: In pattern, 4 repeats and 12 rows = 4"

BODY
Ch 194 **loosely**.
Row 1: Sc in second ch from hook and in each ch across: 193 sc.
To work **Shell**, dc in next sc, (ch 1, dc in same st) twice.
Row 2 (Right side)**:** Ch 1, turn; sc in first sc, ★ skip next 2 sc, work Shell, skip next 2 sc, sc in next sc; repeat from ★ across: 32 Shells.

Row 3: Ch 5 **(counts as first dc plus ch 2, now and throughout)**, turn; skip next dc, sc in next dc, ch 2, skip next dc, dc in next sc, ★ ch 2, skip next dc, sc in next dc, ch 2, skip next dc, dc in next sc; repeat from ★ across: 64 ch-2 sps.
Row 4: Ch 1, turn; sc in first dc, (work Shell, sc in next dc) across: 32 Shells.
Row 5: Ch 5, turn; skip next dc, sc in next dc, ch 2, skip next dc, dc in next sc, ★ ch 2, skip next dc, sc in next dc, ch 2, skip next dc, dc in next sc; repeat from ★ across: 64 ch-2 sps.
Repeat Rows 4 and 5 until Afghan measures approximately 44" from beginning ch, ending by working Row 4.
Last Row: Ch 1, turn; sc in each st and in each ch-1 sp across; do **not** finish off: 193 sc.

EDGING
Rnd 1: Ch 1, turn; 2 sc in first sc, skip next sc, sc in each sc across to last 2 sc, skip next sc, 3 sc in last sc; work 243 sc evenly spaced across end of rows; working in free loops of beginning ch **(Fig. 23b, page 125)**, 3 sc in ch at base of first sc, skip next ch, sc in each ch across to last 2 chs, skip next ch, 3 sc in last ch; work 243 sc evenly spaced across end of rows, sc in same st as first sc; join with slip st to first sc: 876 sc.
Rnd 2: Ch 3, do **not** turn; 4 dc in same st, skip next 2 sc, sc in next sc, skip next 2 sc, ★ 5 dc in next sc, skip next 2 sc, sc in next sc, skip next 2 sc; repeat from ★ around; join with slip st to top of beginning ch-3: 146 5-dc groups.
Rnd 3: Turn; working in Front Loops Only **(Fig. 22, page 125)**, slip st in first sc, sc in next 5 dc, (slip st in next sc, sc in next 5 sts) around; join with slip st to first slip st, finish off.

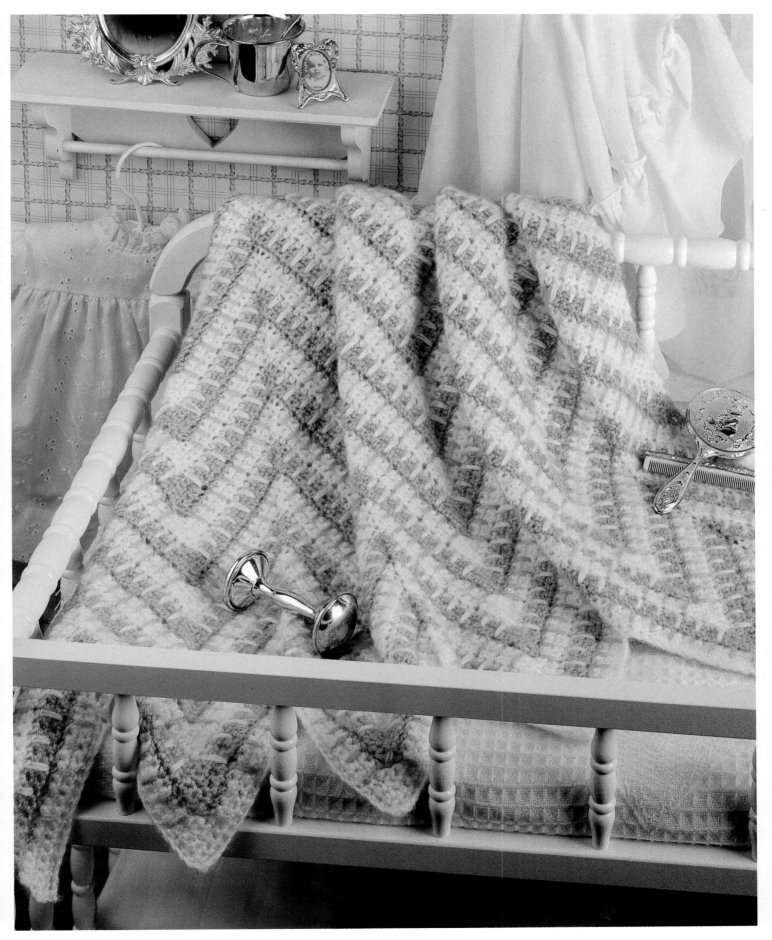

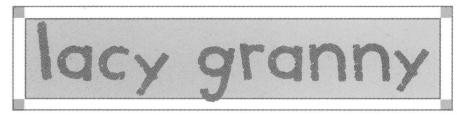

Decidedly dainty, the granny squares in this frilly throw get their lacy look from V-stitches. The airy edging and ribbon trim enhance the feminine flair.

Finished Size: Approximately 36" x 45"

MATERIALS
Sport Weight Yarn, approximately:
  MC (White) - 11 ounces,
    (310 grams, 1,040 yards)
  Color A (Green) - 1½ ounces,
    (40 grams, 140 yards)
  Color B (Peach) - 3 ounces,
    (90 grams, 285 yards)
Crochet hook, size F (3.75 mm) **or** size needed
  for gauge
7 yards of ⅜" wide ribbon
Yarn needle

GAUGE: Each Square = 4¼"

SQUARE (Make 63)
Rnd 1 (Right side): With Color A, ch 4, 2 dc in fourth ch from hook, ch 3, (3 dc in same st, ch 3) 3 times; join with slip st to top of beginning ch, finish off: 4 ch-3 sps.
Note: Loop a short piece of yarn around any stitch to mark last round as **right** side.
Rnd 2: With **right** side facing, join Color B with slip st in any ch-3 sp; ch 3 **(counts as first dc, now and throughout)**, (2 dc, ch 3, 3 dc) in same sp, ch 1, ★ (3 dc, ch 3, 3 dc) in next ch-3 sp, ch 1; repeat from ★ around; join with slip st to first dc, finish off: 24 dc.
To work **V-St**, (dc, ch 3, dc) in st or sp indicated.
Rnd 3: With **right** side facing, join MC with slip st in any ch-3 sp; ch 6 **(counts as first dc plus ch 3, now and throughout)**, (dc, ch 5, work V-St) in same sp, ch 1, work V-St in next ch-1 sp, ch 1, ★ work (V-St, ch 5, V-St) in next ch-3 sp, ch 1, work V-St in next ch-1 sp, ch 1; repeat from ★ around; join with slip st to first dc: 12 V-Sts.
Rnd 4: Slip st in first ch-3 sp, ch 3, 2 dc in same sp, (3 dc, ch 3, 3 dc) in next loop, ★ 3 dc in each of next 3 V-Sts (ch-3 sp), (3 dc, ch 3, 3 dc) in next loop; repeat from ★ 2 times **more**, 3 dc in each of last 2 V-Sts; join with slip st to first dc, finish off.

ASSEMBLY
With **wrong** sides together and MC, and working through **both** loops, whipstitch Squares together forming 7 vertical strips of 9 Squares each **(Fig. 25a, page 126)**; then whipstitch strips together securing seam at each joining.

EDGING
Rnd 1: With **right** side facing, join MC with slip st in any corner ch-3 sp; ch 3, (dc, ch 3, 2 dc) in same sp, dc in next 15 dc, † dc in next sp and in next joining, dc in next sp and in next 15 dc †, repeat from † to † across to next corner ch-3 sp, ★ (2 dc, ch 3, 2 dc) in ch-3 sp, dc in next 15 dc, repeat from † to † across to next ch-3 sp; repeat from ★ around; join with slip st to first dc: 580 dc.
Rnd 2: Slip st in next dc and first ch-3 sp, ch 1, (sc, ch 3, sc) in same sp, ch 1, ★ (skip next dc, sc in next dc, ch 1) across to within one dc of next ch-3 sp, skip next dc, (sc, ch 3, sc) in next ch-3 sp, ch 1; repeat from ★ 2 times **more**, (skip next dc, sc in next dc, ch 1) across to last dc, skip last dc; join with slip st to first sc: 296 sc.
Rnd 3 (Eyelet rnd): Ch 3, (dc, ch 5, dc) in next ch-3 sp, ★ dc in next sc, (ch 1, dc in next sc) across to next ch-3 sp, (dc, ch 5, dc) in ch-3 sp; repeat from ★ 2 times **more**, (dc in next sc, ch 1) across; join with slip st to first dc: 304 dc.
Rnd 4: Ch 6, dc in same st, ch 1, work (V-St, ch 5, V-St) in next loop, ch 1, ★ (skip next dc, work V-St in next dc, ch 1) across to within one dc of next loop, skip next dc, work (V-St, ch 5, V-St) in loop, ch 1; repeat from ★ 2 times **more**, (skip next dc, work V-St in next dc, ch 1) across to last dc, skip last dc; join with slip st to first dc: 158 V-Sts.
Rnd 5: Slip st in first ch-3 sp, ch 6, dc in same sp, ch 1, work V-St in next V-St, ch 1, (dc, ch 5, dc) in next loop, ch 1, ★ (work V-St in next V-St, ch 1) across to next loop, (dc, ch 5, dc) in loop, ch 1; repeat from ★ 2 times **more**, (work V-St in next V-St, ch 1) across; join with slip st to first dc.
To work **Lace St**, ch 3, dc in third ch from hook.

Rnd 6: Slip st in first ch-3 sp, ch 6, dc in third ch from hook, dc in same sp, ch 1, (dc, work Lace St, dc) in next V-St, ch 1, dc in next loop, (work Lace St, dc in same sp) 3 times, ch 1, ★ **[**(dc, work Lace St, dc) in next V-St, ch 1**]** across to next loop, dc in next loop, (work Lace St, dc in same sp) 3 times, ch 1; repeat from ★ 2 times **more**, **[**(dc, work Lace St, dc) in next V-St, ch 1**]** across; join with slip st to first dc, finish off.

FINISHING

Weave ribbon through Eyelet rnd along each side of Afghan, leaving 10" at each end. Tie ends in a bow at each corner.

59

puff parade

Worked all in one piece using sport weight yarn, this cuddly afghan gets its texture from a parade of simple puff stitches. A pretty picot edging adds charm.

Finished Size: Approximately 35" x 47"

MATERIALS
Sport Weight Yarn, approximately:
  18½ ounces, (530 grams, 1,745 yards)
Crochet hook, size G (4.00 mm) **or** size needed for gauge

GAUGE: In pattern, 8 dc and 4 Puff Sts = 4½"
  10 rows = 4½"

Gauge Swatch: (6¾" x 4½")
Ch 27 **loosely**.
Work same as Afghan for 10 rows.
Finish off.

BODY
Ch 129 **loosely**.
To work **Puff St**, ★ YO, insert hook in st indicated, YO and pull up a loop even with loop on hook; repeat from ★ 2 times **more**, YO and draw through all 7 loops on hook *(Fig. 17, page 123)*, ch 1 to close.
Row 1: Dc in fourth ch from hook and in next 6 chs, ★ ch 1, (skip next ch, work Puff St in next ch) 4 times, ch 1, skip next ch, dc in next 8 chs; repeat from ★ across: 28 Puff Sts.
Row 2 (Right side)**:** Ch 3 **(counts as first dc, now and throughout)**, turn; dc in next 7 dc, ch 1, work Puff St in ch-1 closing of each of next 4 Puff Sts, ch 1, ★ dc in next 8 dc, ch 1, work Puff St in ch-1 closing of each of next 4 Puff Sts, ch 1; repeat from ★ 5 times **more**, dc in next 7 dc and in top of beginning ch: 64 dc.
Note: Loop a short piece of yarn around any stitch to mark last row as **right** side.
Row 3: Ch 3, turn; dc in next 7 dc, ★ ch 1, work Puff St in ch-1 closing of each of next 4 Puff Sts, ch 1, dc in next 8 dc; repeat from ★ across.
Repeat Row 3 for pattern until Afghan measures approximately 45" from beginning ch, ending by working a **wrong** side row; do **not** finish off.

EDGING
Rnd 1: Ch 1, turn; sc in first 8 dc and in next ch-1 sp, sc in ch-1 closing of next Puff St, (sc in sp **before** next Puff St and in ch-1 closing of next Puff St) 3 times, sc in next ch-1 sp, ★ sc in next 8 dc and in next ch-1 sp, sc in ch-1 closing of next Puff St, (sc in sp **before** next Puff St and in ch-1 closing of next Puff St) 3 times, sc in next ch-1 sp; repeat from ★ 5 times **more**, sc in next 7 dc, 3 sc in last dc; work 158 sc evenly spaced across end of rows; working in free loops of beginning ch *(Fig. 23b, page 125)*, 3 sc in ch at base of first st, sc in next 125 chs, 3 sc in last ch; work 158 sc evenly spaced across end of rows, 2 sc in same dc as first sc; join with slip st to first sc: 578 sc.
To work **Picot**, ch 4, sc in third ch from hook.

Rnd 2: Ch 1, do **not** turn; sc in same st, work Picot, ch 2, ★ † (skip next 2 sc, sc in next sc, work Picot, ch 2) across to center sc of next corner, skip next sc †, sc in next sc, work Picot, ch 2; repeat from ★ 2 times **more**, then repeat from † to † once; join with slip st to first sc, finish off.

itsy bitsy spiderweb

Single and treble crochet stitches and chain loops form the delicate spiderweb pattern on this light and airy afghan. The sport weight cover-up will make a comforting wrap at lullaby time!

Finished Size: Approximately 34" x 46½"

MATERIALS

Sport Weight Yarn, approximately:
13 ounces, (370 grams, 1,255 yards)
Crochet hook, size H (5.00 mm) **or** size needed
for gauge

GAUGE: 16 dc and 10 rows = 4"

BODY

Ch 137 **loosely**.

Row 1: Dc in fourth ch from hook and in each ch across: 135 sts.

Row 2 (Right side)**:** Ch 3 **(counts as first dc, now and throughout)**, turn; dc in next 2 dc, ★ ch 1, skip next dc, dc in next 15 dc; repeat from ★ across to last 4 dc, ch 1, skip next dc, dc in last 3 dc.

Note: Loop a short piece of yarn around any stitch to mark last row as **right** side.

Row 3: Ch 3, turn; dc in next 2 dc, ch 1, ★ dc in next dc, (ch 1, skip next dc, dc in next dc) 7 times, ch 1; repeat from ★ across to last 3 dc, dc in last 3 dc.

Row 4: Ch 3, turn; dc in next 2 dc, ch 1, ★ dc in next dc, (dc in next ch-1 sp and in next dc) 7 times, ch 1; repeat from ★ across to last 3 dc, dc in last 3 dc.

Row 5: Ch 3, turn; dc in next 2 dc, ch 1, ★ dc in next 15 dc, ch 1; repeat from ★ across to last 3 dc, dc in last 3 dc.

Row 6: Ch 3, turn; dc in next 2 dc, ch 1, ★ dc in next 3 dc, ch 3, (skip next dc, tr in next dc) 4 times, ch 3, skip next dc, dc in next 3 dc, ch 1; repeat from ★ across to last 3 dc, dc in last 3 dc.

Row 7: Ch 3, turn; dc in next 2 dc, ch 1, ★ dc in next 3 dc, ch 3, sc in next 4 tr, ch 3, dc in next 3 dc, ch 1; repeat from ★ across to last 3 dc, dc in last 3 dc.

Rows 8-10: Ch 3, turn; dc in next 2 dc, ch 1, ★ dc in next 3 dc, ch 3, sc in next 4 sc, ch 3, dc in next 3 dc, ch 1; repeat from ★ across to last 3 dc, dc in last 3 dc.

Row 11: Ch 3, turn; dc in next 2 dc, ch 1, ★ dc in next 3 dc, ch 1, (tr in next sc, ch 1) 4 times, dc in next 3 dc, ch 1; repeat from ★ across to last 3 dc, dc in last 3 dc.

Row 12: Ch 3, turn; dc in next 2 dc, ch 1, ★ dc in next 3 dc and in next ch-1 sp, (dc in next tr and in next ch-1 sp) 4 times, dc in next 3 dc, ch 1; repeat from ★ across to last 3 dc, dc in last 3 dc.

Row 13: Repeat Row 5.

Rows 14-114: Repeat Rows 3-13, 9 times; then repeat Rows 3 and 4 once **more**.

Row 115: Ch 3, turn; dc in next dc and in each dc and each ch-1 sp across, do **not** finish off.

EDGING

Rnd 1: Ch 1, turn; work 136 sc evenly spaced across; working in end of rows, 3 sc in first row, work 173 sc evenly spaced across to last row, 3 sc in last row; working in free loops of beginning ch *(Fig. 23b, page 125)*, work 136 sc evenly spaced across; working in end of rows, 3 sc in first row, work 173 sc evenly spaced across to last row, 3 sc in last row; join with slip st to first sc: 630 sc.

Rnd 2: Ch 1, ★ sc in next sc, ch 4, sc in third ch from hook, ch 2, skip next 2 sc; repeat from ★ around; join with slip st to first sc, finish off.

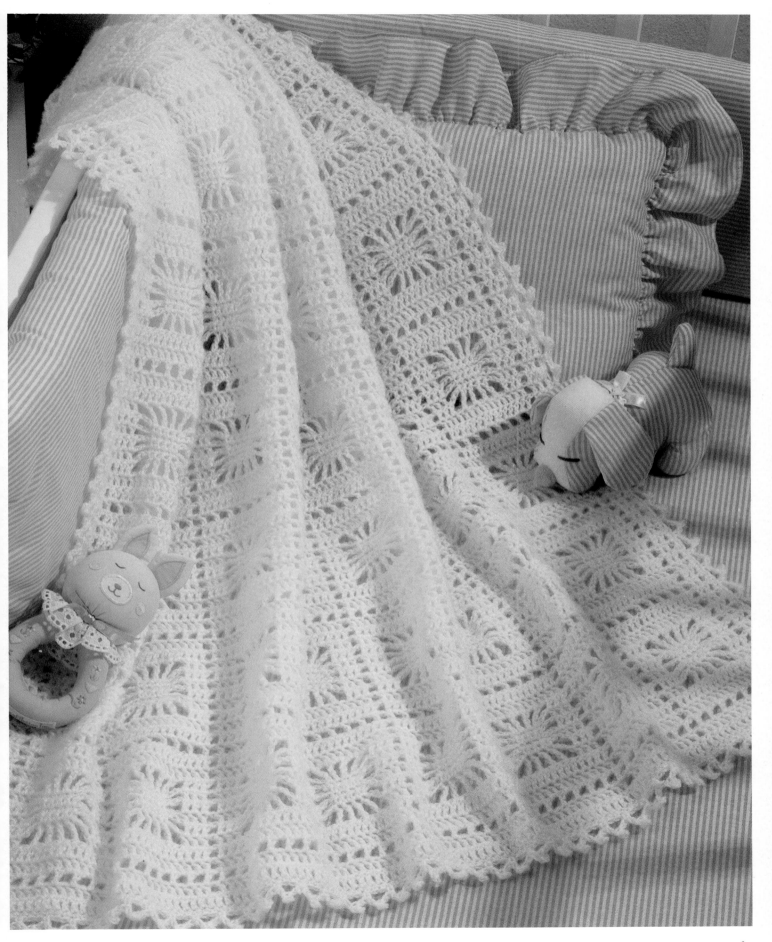

gentle caress

Fashioned from baby fingering weight yarn, this mile-a-minute afghan will caress your favorite little lamb with softness. The foundation of lacy shell stitches is worked with a large hook and bordered by rows of double crochet and chain stitches worked with a smaller hook.

Finished Size: Approximately 30" x 46"

MATERIALS
Baby Fingering Weight Yarn, approximately:
MC (Off-White) - 6 ounces,
(170 grams, 860 yards)
Color A (Pink) - 3 ounces, (90 grams, 430 yards)
Color B (Green) - 3½ ounces,
(100 grams, 500 yards)
Crochet hooks, sizes D (3.25 mm) **and**
F (3.75 mm) **or** sizes needed for gauge
Yarn needle

GAUGE: With larger size hook, Rows 1-7 = 4"
With smaller size hook, 28 dc = 4"
One Strip = 2¾" wide

STRIP (Make 11)
CENTER
To work **Shell**, (3 dc, ch 1, 3 dc) in st or sp indicated.
With MC and larger size hook, ch 4 **loosely**.
Foundation (Right side): (2 Dc, ch 1, 3 dc) in fourth ch from hook, ch 3; working in free loops of beginning ch **(Fig. 23b, page 125)**, work Shell in first ch, skip next 2 chs, dc in last ch; do **not** finish off.
Note: Loop a short piece of yarn around any stitch to mark Foundation as **right** side and bottom edge.
Row 1: Ch 3 **(counts as first dc, now and throughout)**, turn; work Shell in next ch-1 sp, skip next 3 dc, dc in next ch: 8 dc.
Rows 2-75: Ch 3, turn; work Shell in next ch-1 sp, skip next 3 dc, dc in last dc.
Finish off.

BORDER
Rnd 1: With **right** side facing and using smaller size hook, join Color A with slip st in ch-1 sp on Row 75; ch 3, (4 dc, ch 2, 5 dc) in same sp, ch 2; working in end of rows, 3 dc in first row, ch 1, (3 dc in next row, ch 1) across to Foundation; working in Foundation, 3 dc in first sp, ch 2, (5 dc, ch 2, 5 dc) in next ch-1 sp, ch 2, 3 dc in last sp, ch 1; working in end of rows, 3 dc in first row, (ch 1, 3 dc in next row) across, ch 2; join with slip st to first dc, finish off: 476 dc.
Rnd 2: With **right** side facing and using smaller size hook, join Color B with slip st in same st as joining; ch 3, dc in next 4 dc, † work Shell in next ch-2 sp, dc in next 5 dc, 2 dc in next ch-2 sp, dc in next dc, place marker around dc just made for joining placement, dc in next dc and in each dc and each ch-1 sp across to next ch-2 sp, place marker around last dc made for joining placement, 2 dc in ch-2 sp †, dc in next 5 dc, repeat from † to † once; join with slip st to first dc, finish off.

ASSEMBLY
With **wrong** sides together and Color B, and working through **inside** loops only, whipstitch two Strips together beginning in first marked dc and ending in next marked dc **(Fig. 25b, page 126)**; then whipstitch remaining Strips together.

wee irish chain

Bundle up your bonny babe in our pretty afghan inspired by the Irish Chain quilt pattern. Crocheted in soft pastels, it will keep your wee one warm and comfy at naptime.

Finished Size: Approximately 33" x 33"

MATERIALS
Sport Weight Yarn, approximately:
  MC (White) - 11 ounces,
    (310 grams, 1,100 yards)
  CC (Green) - 9 ounces, (260 grams, 900 yards)
Crochet hook, size G (4.00 mm) **or** size needed for
  gauge

GAUGE: 4 Blocks = 3"
      Rows 1-5 = 3¾" x 3¾" x 5"
      (triangle)

Note: Afghan is worked diagonally.

PATTERN STITCHES
BEGINNING BLOCK
Ch 6 **loosely**, turn; dc in fourth ch from hook and
in next 2 chs.
BLOCK
Slip st in ch-3 sp on next Block, ch 3, 3 dc in same
sp.

BODY
Row 1: With MC, ch 6 **loosely**, dc in fourth ch from
hook and in next 2 chs: 1 Block.
Row 2 (Right side)**:** Work Beginning Block, slip st in
ch-3 sp on previous Block *(Fig. 1a)*, ch 3, 3 dc in
same sp *(Fig. 1b)*: 2 Blocks.

Fig. 1a

Fig. 1b

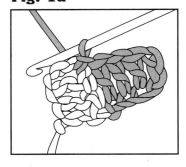
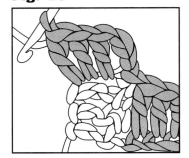

Note: Loop a short piece of yarn around any stitch
to mark last row as **right** side.
Row 3: Work Beginning Block, slip st in ch-3 sp on
first Block, ch 3, 3 dc in same sp, work Block:
3 Blocks.
Row 4: Work Beginning Block, slip st in ch-3 sp on
first Block, ch 3, 3 dc in same sp, work Blocks
across: 4 Blocks.
Row 5: Work Beginning Block, slip st in ch-3 sp on
first Block, ch 3, 3 dc in same sp, work Blocks
across changing to CC in last dc *(Fig. 21a, page
125)*: 5 Blocks.
Note: Always change colors in same manner. Keep
unused color to **wrong** side of work; do **not** cut yarn
until color is no longer needed.
When working vertical Blocks of CC, use a separate
skein for each set of Blocks.
Row 6: With CC, work Beginning Block, slip st in
ch-3 sp on first Block, ch 3, 3 dc in same sp, work
Blocks across: 6 Blocks.
Row 7: With MC, work Beginning Block, slip st in
ch-3 sp on first Block, ch 3, 3 dc in same sp, work
Blocks across: 7 Blocks.
Rows 8 and 9: Repeat Rows 6 and 7: 9 Blocks.
Row 10: Work Beginning Block, with CC slip st in
ch-3 sp on first Block, ch 3, 3 dc in same sp, work
Block, with MC work 4 Blocks, with CC work
2 Blocks, with MC work last Block: 10 Blocks.
Row 11: Repeat Row 7: 11 Blocks.
Row 12: Work Beginning Block, slip st in ch-3 sp
on first Block, ch 3, 3 dc in same sp, with CC work
2 Blocks, with MC work 4 Blocks, with CC work
2 Blocks, with MC work last 2 Blocks: 12 Blocks.
Row 13: Repeat Row 7: 13 Blocks.
Row 14: Work Beginning Block, slip st in ch-3 sp
on first Block, ch 3, 3 dc in same sp, work Block,
with CC work 2 Blocks, with MC work 4 Blocks,
with CC work 2 Blocks, with MC work last 3 Blocks:
14 Blocks.
Row 15: Repeat Row 7: 15 Blocks.

Row 16: Work Beginning Block, slip st in ch-3 sp on first Block, ch 3, 3 dc in same sp, work 2 Blocks, (with CC work 2 Blocks, with MC work 4 Blocks) twice: 16 Blocks.

Rows 17-21: Repeat Rows 5-9: 21 Blocks.

Row 22: Work Beginning Block, with CC slip st in ch-3 sp on first Block, ch 3, 3 dc in same sp, work Block, (with MC work 4 Blocks, with CC work 2 Blocks) across to last Block, with MC work last Block: 22 Blocks.

Row 23: Repeat Row 7: 23 Blocks.

Row 24: Work Beginning Block, slip st in ch-3 sp on first Block, ch 3, 3 dc in same sp, with CC work 2 Blocks, (with MC work 4 Blocks, with CC work 2 Blocks) across to last 2 Blocks, with MC work last 2 Blocks: 24 Blocks.

Row 25: Repeat Row 7: 25 Blocks.

Row 26: Work Beginning Block, slip st in ch-3 sp on first Block, ch 3, 3 dc in same sp, work Block, with CC work 2 Blocks, (with MC work 4 Blocks, with CC work 2 Blocks) across to last 3 Blocks, with MC work last 3 Blocks: 26 Blocks.

Row 27: Repeat Row 7: 27 Blocks.

Row 28: Work Beginning Block, slip st in ch-3 sp on first Block, ch 3, 3 dc in same sp, work 2 Blocks, (with CC work 2 Blocks, with MC work 4 Blocks) across: 28 Blocks.

Rows 29-37: Repeat Rows 17-25: 37 Blocks.

Row 38: Turn; slip st in first 3 dc and in first ch-3 sp, ch 3, 3 dc in same sp, work Block, with CC work 2 Blocks, (with MC work 4 Blocks, with CC work 2 Blocks) across to last 3 Blocks, with MC work 2 Blocks, slip st in ch-3 sp on last Block: 36 Blocks.

Row 39: Turn; slip st in first 3 dc and in first ch-3 sp, ch 3, 3 dc in same sp, work Blocks across to last Block, slip st in ch-3 sp on last Block: 35 Blocks.

Row 40: Turn; slip st in first 3 dc and in first ch-3 sp, ch 3, 3 dc in same sp, with CC work 2 Blocks, (with MC work 4 Blocks, with CC work 2 Blocks) across to last 2 Blocks, with MC work Block, slip st in ch-3 sp on last Block: 34 Blocks.

Row 41: Repeat Row 39: 33 Blocks.

Row 42: Turn; with CC slip st in first 3 dc and in first ch-3 sp, ch 3, 3 dc in same sp, work Blocks across to last Block, slip st in ch-3 sp on last Block: 32 Blocks.

Row 43: Turn; with MC slip st in first 3 dc and in first ch-3 sp, ch 3, 3 dc in same sp, work Blocks across to last Block, slip st in ch-3 sp on last Block: 31 Blocks.

Rows 44 and 45: Repeat Rows 42 and 43: 29 Blocks.

Row 46: Turn; slip st in first 3 dc and in first ch-3 sp, ch 3, 3 dc in same sp, work 3 Blocks, (with CC work 2 Blocks, with MC work 4 Blocks) across to last Block, slip st in ch-3 sp on last Block: 28 Blocks.

Row 47: Repeat Row 39: 27 Blocks.
Row 48: Turn; slip st in first 3 dc and in first ch-3 sp, ch 3, 3 dc in same sp, work 2 Blocks, with CC work 2 Blocks, (with MC work 4 Blocks, with CC work 2 Blocks) across to last 4 Blocks, with MC work 3 Blocks, slip st in ch-3 sp on last Block: 26 Blocks.
Row 49: Repeat Row 39: 25 Blocks.
Rows 50-57: Repeat Rows 38-45: 17 Blocks.
Row 58: Turn; Slip st in first 3 dc and in first ch-3 sp, ch 3, 3 dc in same sp, work 3 Blocks, (with CC work 2 Blocks, with MC work 4 Blocks) twice, slip st in ch-3 sp on last Block: 16 Blocks.
Row 59: Repeat Row 39: 15 Blocks.
Row 60: Turn; slip st in first 3 dc and in first ch-3 sp, ch 3, 3 dc in same sp, work 2 Blocks, with CC work 2 Blocks, with MC work 4 Blocks, with CC work 2 Blocks, with MC work 3 Blocks, slip st in ch-3 sp on last Block: 14 Blocks.
Row 61: Repeat Row 39: 13 Blocks.
Row 62: Turn; slip st in first 3 dc and in first ch-3 sp, ch 3, 3 dc in same sp, work Block, with CC work 2 Blocks, with MC work 4 Blocks, with CC work 2 Blocks, with MC work 2 Blocks, slip st in ch-3 sp on last Block: 12 Blocks.
Row 63: Repeat Row 39: 11 Blocks.
Row 64: Turn; slip st in first 3 dc and in first ch-3 sp, ch 3, 3 dc in same sp, with CC work 2 Blocks, with MC work 4 Blocks, with CC work 2 Blocks, with MC work Block, slip st in ch-3 sp on last Block: 10 Blocks.
Row 65: Repeat Row 39: 9 Blocks.
Rows 66-69: Repeat Rows 42-45: 5 Blocks.

Rows 70-72: Turn; slip st in first 3 dc and in first ch-3 sp, ch 3, 3 dc in same sp, work Blocks across to last Block, slip st in ch-3 sp on last Block: 2 Blocks.
Row 73: Turn; slip st in first 3 dc and in first ch-3 sp, ch 3, 3 dc in same sp, slip st in ch-3 sp on last Block; do **not** finish off: 1 Block.

EDGING
Rnd 1: Ch 1, turn; sc in sp **between** Blocks, ch 2, sc in corner, ch 2, ★ (sc in next sp **between** Blocks, ch 2) across to corner, sc in corner, ch 2; repeat from ★ 2 times **more**, (sc in sp **between** Blocks, ch 2) across; join with slip st to first sc, finish off: 37 ch-2 sps **each** side.
Rnd 2: With **right** side facing, join CC with slip st in ch-2 sp to left of any corner; ch 3, 2 dc in same sp, (3 dc in each ch-2 sp across to next corner, ch 3) around; join with slip st to top of beginning ch-3.
Rnds 3-5: Ch 3, working in Back Loops Only **(Fig. 22, page 125)**, dc in next dc and in each dc around working (3 dc, ch 3, 3 dc) in each corner ch-3 sp; join with slip st to top of beginning ch-3.
Rnd 6: Ch 3, working in Back Loops Only, dc in next dc and in each dc around working (2 dc, ch 2, 2 dc) in each corner ch-3 sp; join with slip st to top of beginning ch-3, finish off.
Rnd 7: With **right** side facing, join MC with slip st in same st as joining; ch 3, working in Back Loops Only, dc in next dc and in each dc around working (2 dc, ch 2, 2 dc) in each corner ch-2 sp; join with slip st to top of beginning ch-3.
Rnd 8: Ch 1, work reverse sc in both loops of next dc and in each dc and each ch around **(Figs. 18a-d, page 124)**; join with slip st to first st, finish off.

Featuring bands of pastel stripes, this huggable afghan is crocheted using brushed acrylic worsted weight yarn. Lush fringe finishes the wrap.

Finished Size: Approximately 38" x 51"

MATERIALS
Worsted Weight Brushed Acrylic Yarn, approximately:
    MC (White) - 10 ounces,
      (280 grams, 770 yards)
    Color A (Pink) - 9 ounces,
      (260 grams, 695 yards)
    Color B (Blue) - 3½ ounces,
      (100 grams, 270 yards)
    Color C (Yellow) - 3½ ounces,
      (100 grams, 270 yards)
    Color D (Mint) - 3½ ounces,
      (100 grams, 270 yards)
Crochet hook, size I (5.50 mm) **or** size needed for gauge

GAUGE: In pattern, 3 repeats = 3½"
and 8 rows = 4"

BODY

With Color A, ch 232 **loosely**.
Row 1: 2 Dc in fourth ch from hook **(3 skipped chs count as first dc)**, skip next 3 chs, sc in next ch, ★ ch 3, dc in next 3 chs, skip next 3 chs, sc in next ch; repeat from ★ across: 132 sts and 32 ch-3 sps.

Row 2 (Right side)**:** Ch 3 **(counts as first dc, now and throughout)**, turn; 2 dc in same st, ★ skip next 3 dc, (sc, ch 3, 2 dc) in next ch-3 sp, dc in next sc; repeat from ★ across to last 3 dc, skip next 2 dc, sc in last dc: 99 dc.
Note: Loop a short piece of yarn around any stitch to mark last row as **right** side.
Rows 3-101: Ch 3, turn; 2 dc in same st, ★ skip next 3 dc, (sc, ch 3, 2 dc) in next ch-3 sp, dc in next sc; repeat from ★ across to last 3 dc, skip next 2 dc, sc in last dc.
Finish off.

FRINGE

Using six 18" strands, add fringe in each ch-3 sp across short edges of Afghan *(Figs. 26a & b, page 126)*.

woven stripes

This cozy throw is easy to make using single crochets and chain spaces. The woven-look stripes are worked across the length of the afghan, creating the matching fringe as you go.

Finished Size: Approximately 32" x 44"

MATERIALS

Sport Weight Yarn, approximately:
- MC (White) - 9½ ounces,
  (270 grams, 895 yards)
- Color A (Pink) - 2½ ounces,
  (70 grams, 235 yards)
- Color B (Green) - 2½ ounces,
  (70 grams, 235 yards)
- Color C (Yellow) - 2½ ounces,
  (70 grams, 235 yards)
- Color D (Blue) - 2½ ounces,
  (70 grams, 235 yards)
- Crochet hook, size H (5.00 mm) **or** size needed for gauge

GAUGE: In pattern, (ch 1, sc) 9 times
and 18 rows = 4"

Note: Each row is worked across length of Afghan.

STRIPE SEQUENCE

STRIPE SEQUENCE
One row **each** color: Color A, ★ MC, Color B, MC, Color C, MC, Color D, MC, Color A; repeat from ★ throughout.

BODY

With Color A and leaving a 7" end for fringe, ch 198 **loosely**.

Row 1 (Right side)**:** Sc in second ch from hook, ★ ch 1, skip next ch, sc in next ch; repeat from ★ across; finish off leaving a 7" end for fringe: 99 sc and 98 ch-1 sps.

Note: Loop a short piece of yarn around any stitch to mark last row as **right** side.

Row 2: With **wrong** side facing and leaving a 7" end for fringe, join next color with sc in first sc **(see Joining with Sc, page 125)**; sc in next ch-1 sp, (ch 1, sc in next ch-1 sp) across to last sc, sc in last sc; finish off leaving a 7" end for fringe: 100 sc and 97 ch-1 sps.

Row 3: With **right** side facing and leaving a 7" end for fringe, join next color with sc in first sc; ch 1, (sc in next ch-1 sp, ch 1) across to last 2 sc, skip next sc, sc in last sc; finish off leaving a 7" end for fringe: 99 sc and 98 ch-1 sps.

Repeat Rows 2 and 3 until Afghan measures approximately 32" from beginning ch, ending by using Color A.

FRINGE

Using one 15" length of corresponding color, add fringe in end of each row across **(Figs. 26c & d, page 126)**.

gentle waves

Light and airy, this easy-to-crochet throw is perfect for warm weather. The mile-a-minute pattern is crocheted in blue and white to resemble frothy ocean waves.

Finished Size: Approximately 32" x 44"

MATERIALS
Sport Weight Yarn, approximately:
  MC (Blue) - 5½ ounces, (160 grams, 550 yards)
  CC (White) - 4½ ounces, (130 grams, 450 yards)
Crochet hook, size H (5.00 mm) **or** size needed for gauge

GAUGE: 16 dc and 8 rows = 4"
  One Strip = 3½" wide

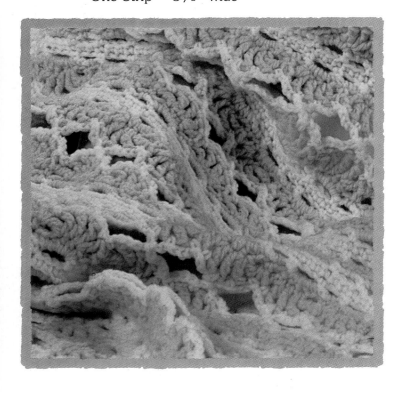

FIRST STRIP
With CC, ch 161 **loosely**.

Foundation Row (Right side)**:** Sc in second ch from hook and in each ch across: 160 sc.

Note: Loop a short piece of yarn around any stitch to mark last row as **right** side.

Rnd 1: Ch 1, (sc, ch 3) twice in end of row; working in free loops of beginning ch *(Fig. 23b, page 125)*, sc in first ch, (ch 3, skip next 2 chs, sc in next ch) across, ch 3, (sc, ch 3) twice in same ch; working across Foundation Row, sc in first sc, ch 3, (skip next 2 sc, sc in next sc, ch 3) across; join with slip st to first sc, finish off: 112 ch-3 sps.

Rnd 2: With **right** side facing, join MC with slip st in center ch-3 sp on either end; ch 1, (sc, 6 hdc, sc) in same sp, † ch 1, sc in next ch-3 sp, ch 1, ★ (sc, 3 hdc, sc) in next ch-3 sp, ch 1, sc in next ch-3 sp, ch 1; repeat from ★ 26 times **more** †, (sc, 6 hdc, sc) in next ch-3 sp, repeat from † to † once; join with slip st to first sc.

Rnd 3: Ch 4, dc in same st, ch 1, † tr in next hdc, (ch 1, tr) twice in next hdc, skip next hdc, sc in next hdc, (dc, ch 1) twice in next hdc, tr in next hdc, (ch 1, tr) twice in next sc, sc in next sc, ★ skip next sc, (dc, ch 1) twice in next hdc, tr in next hdc, (ch 1, tr) twice in next hdc, skip next sc, sc in next sc; repeat from ★ 26 times **more** †, (dc, ch 1) twice in next sc, repeat from † to † once; join with slip st to third ch of beginning ch-4, finish off.

Rnd 4: With **right** side facing, join CC with slip st in center sc on either end; ch 1, sc in same st, † (ch 3, slip st in last sc worked) 3 times, (ch 3, sc in next ch-1 sp) 4 times, ★ skip next 3 sts, sc in next ch-1 sp, (ch 3, sc in next ch-1 sp) 3 times; repeat from ★ 26 times **more**, skip next 3 sts, (sc in next ch-1 sp, ch 3) 4 times †, sc in next sc, repeat from † to † once; join with slip st to first sc, finish off.

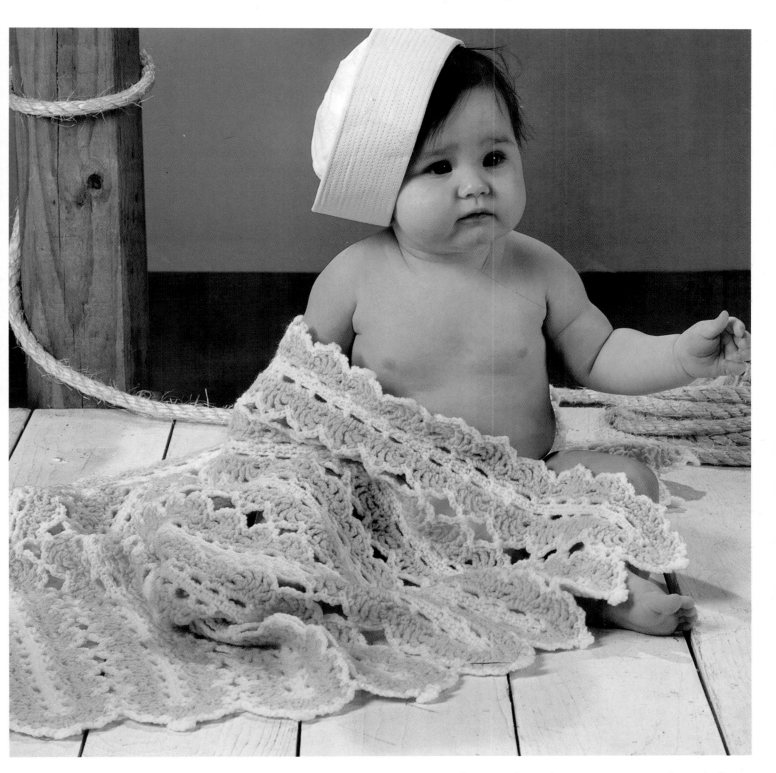

REMAINING 8 STRIPS

Work same as First Strip through Rnd 3.

Rnd 4 (Joining rnd)**:** With **right** side facing, join CC with slip st in center sc on either end; ch 1, sc in same st, (ch 3, slip st in last sc worked) 3 times, (ch 3, sc in next ch-1 sp) 4 times, [skip next 3 sts, sc in next ch-1 sp, (ch 3, sc in next ch-1 sp) 3 times] 27 times, skip next 3 sts, (sc in next ch-1 sp, ch 3) 4 times, sc in next sc, (ch 3, slip st in last sc worked) 3 times, (ch 3, sc in next ch-1 sp) 3 times, ch 1, place Strips with **wrong** sides together, slip st in corresponding ch-3 sp on **previous Strip** *(Fig. 24, page 125)*, ch 1, sc in next ch-1 sp on **new Strip**, skip next 3 sts, sc in next ch-1 sp, ★ ch 3, sc in next ch-1 sp, ch 1, slip st in corresponding ch-3 sp on **previous Strip**, ch 1, sc in next ch-1 sp on **new Strip**, ch 3, sc in next ch-1 sp, skip next 3 sts, sc in next ch-1 sp; repeat from ★ 26 times **more**, ch 1, slip st in corresponding ch-3 sp on **previous Strip**, ch 1, (sc in next ch-1 sp on **new Strip**, ch 3) 3 times; join with slip st to first sc, finish off.

miles of shells

Strips of lacy blue shells are enhanced by simple stitches of white and pink on this easy mile-a-minute afghan. Because the wrap works up quickly with worsted weight yarn, you can make extras to have on hand for baby showers.

Finished Size: Approximately 38" x 50"

MATERIALS
Worsted Weight Yarn, approximately:
   MC (Blue) - 13 ounces, (370 grams, 855 yards)
   Color A (White) - 10 ounces,
     (280 grams, 660 yards)
   Color B (Pink) - 5½ ounces,
     (160 grams, 365 yards)
Crochet hook, size G (4.00 mm) **or** size needed
   for gauge

GAUGE: Center of Strip = 2½" and
        7 rows = 4"
        Each Strip = 3¼" wide

STRIP (Make 10)
CENTER
With MC, ch 12 **loosely**.
Row 1: Dc in sixth ch from hook, skip next 2 chs, (dc, ch 4, dc) in next ch, skip next 2 chs, (dc, ch 2, dc) in last ch: 5 dc.
Row 2 (Right side)**:** Ch 5 **(counts as first dc plus ch 2, now and throughout)**, turn; dc in next ch-2 sp, (4 dc, ch 1, 4 dc) in next ch-4 sp, (dc, ch 2, dc) in last sp.
Note: Loop a short piece of yarn around any stitch to mark last row as **right** side and bottom edge.
Row 3: Ch 5, turn; dc in next ch-2 sp, (dc, ch 4, dc) in next ch-1 sp, (dc, ch 2, dc) in last ch-2 sp.
Rows 4-81: Repeat Rows 2 and 3, 39 times changing to Color A in last dc on Row 81 *(Fig. 21a, page 125)*.

EDGING
Ch 1, turn; (sc, hdc, dc) in first ch-2 sp, (3 tr, dtr, 3 tr) in next ch-4 sp, (dc, hdc, sc) in last ch-2 sp, ch 1 (corner), 2 dc in same sp, ch 1, (2 dc in end of next row, ch 1) across to last sp, 2 dc in last sp, ch 1 (corner), (sc, hdc, dc) in same sp, skip next sp, (3 tr, dtr, 3 tr) in free loop of next ch *(Fig. 23b, page 125)*, skip next sp, (dc, hdc, sc) in last sp, ch 1

(corner), 2 dc in same sp, (ch 1, 2 dc in end of next row) across, ch 1 (corner); join with slip st to first sc, finish off.

ASSEMBLY
Join 2 Strips as follows:
With **wrong** sides together and having top of Strips to the **right**, join Color B with slip st in first corner ch-1 sp on **first Strip**; ch 1, sc in same sp, ch 2, sc in first corner ch-1 sp on **second Strip** *(Fig. 24, page 125)*, ch 2, ★ skip next st on **first Strip**, sc in next st, ch 2, skip next st on **second Strip**, sc in next st, ch 2; repeat from ★ across to within 2 dc of next corner ch-1 sp on **both** Strips, skip next 2 dc on **first Strip**, sc in next corner ch-1 sp, ch 2, skip next 2 dc on **second Strip**, sc in next corner ch-1 sp; finish off. Join remaining Strips in the same manner.

TRIM
Rnd 1: With **right** side facing and bottom edge toward you, join Color B with slip st in top right corner ch-1 sp; ch 1, (sc, ch 1, sc) in same sp, † sc in next 6 sts, (sc, ch 1, sc) in next dtr, sc in next 6 sts, ★ 3 sc in next joining, sc in next 6 sts, (sc, ch 1, sc) in next dtr, sc in next 6 sts; repeat from ★ 8 times **more**, (sc, ch 1, sc) in next corner ch-1 sp, sc in next dc, (ch 1, skip next st, sc in next st) across to within one dc of next corner ch-1 sp, ch 1, skip next dc †, (sc, ch 1, sc) in corner ch-1 sp, repeat from † to † once; join with slip st to first sc: 584 sc.
Rnd 2: Slip st in first corner ch-1 sp, ch 1, (sc, ch 2) twice in same sp, † skip next 2 sc, sc in next sc, (ch 2, skip next sc, sc in next sc) twice, ch 2, skip next sc, (sc, ch 2) twice in next ch-1 sp, ★ skip next sc, sc in next sc, (ch 2, skip next sc, sc in next sc) 7 times, ch 2, skip next sc, (sc, ch 2) twice in next ch-1 sp; repeat from ★ 8 times **more**, skip next sc, sc in next sc, (ch 2, skip next sc, sc in next sc) twice, ch 2, skip next 2 sc, (sc, ch 2) twice in next corner ch-1 sp, (sc in next ch-1 sp, ch 2) across to next corner ch-1 sp †, (sc, ch 2) twice in corner ch-1 sp, repeat from † to † once; join with slip st to first sc, finish off.

rainbow ripples

A rainbow of soft color ripples through this sweet afghan to brighten baby's room. The wrap is created using simple stitches and baby fingering weight yarn.

Finished Size: Approximately 28" x 39"

MATERIALS
Baby Fingering Weight Yarn, approximately:
Main Color (White) - 3½ ounces,
(100 grams, 500 yards)
Color A (Pink) - 1½ ounces,
(40 grams, 215 yards)
Color B (Apricot) - 1½ ounces,
(40 grams, 215 yards)
Color C (Yellow) - 1½ ounces,
(40 grams, 215 yards)
Color D (Mint) - 1½ ounces,
(40 grams, 215 yards)
Color E (Blue) - 1½ ounces,
(40 grams, 215 yards)
Crochet hook, size D (3.25 mm) **or** size needed
for gauge

GAUGE: In pattern, 30 sts and 15 rows = 5"

Gauge Swatch: (5" x 5")
Ch 33 **loosely**.
Work same as Afghan for 15 rows.

BODY
With Color A, ch 168 **loosely**.
Row 1: 2 Dc in fourth ch from hook, dc in next 5 chs, skip next 2 chs, dc in next 6 chs, ★ 3 dc in next ch, dc in next 6 chs, skip next 2 chs, dc in next 6 chs; repeat from ★ across to last ch, 2 dc in last ch: 166 sts.
Row 2 (Right side)**:** Ch 3 **(counts as first dc, now and throughout)**, turn; working in Back Loops Only **(Fig. 22, page 125)**, 2 dc in next dc, dc in next 5 dc, skip next 2 dc, dc in next 6 dc, ★ 3 dc in next dc, dc in next 6 dc, skip next 2 dc, dc in next 6 dc; repeat from ★ across to last st, 2 dc in last st.
Note: Loop a short piece of yarn around any stitch to mark last row as **right** side.
Row 3: Repeat Row 2; finish off.

Row 4: With **right** side facing and working in both loops, join MC with slip st in first dc; slip st in each dc across, changing to Color B in last slip st *(Fig. 21a, page 125)*.
Row 5: Ch 3, turn; working in Back Loops Only of dc one row **below** slip sts, 2 dc in next dc, dc in next 5 dc, skip next 2 dc, dc in next 6 dc, ★ 3 dc in next dc, dc in next 6 dc, skip next 2 dc, dc in next 6 dc; repeat from ★ across to last dc, 2 dc in last dc.
Rows 6 and 7: Repeat Row 2 twice; at the end of Row 7, finish off.
Row 8: Repeat Row 4, changing to Color C in last slip st.
Rows 9-11: Repeat Rows 5-7.
Row 12: Repeat Row 4, changing to Color D in last slip st.
Rows 13-15: Repeat Rows 5-7.
Row 16: Repeat Row 4, changing to Color E in last slip st.
Rows 17-19: Repeat Rows 5-7.
Row 20: With **right** side facing and working in both loops, join MC with slip st in first dc, slip st in each dc across.
Rows 21-23: Repeat Rows 5-7.
Row 24: With Color A, repeat Row 4, changing to MC in last slip st.
Rows 25-27: Repeat Rows 5-7.
Row 28: With Color B, repeat Row 4, changing to MC in last slip st.
Rows 29-31: Repeat Rows 5-7.
Row 32: With Color C, repeat Row 4, changing to MC in last slip st.
Rows 33-35: Repeat Rows 5-7.
Row 36: With Color D, repeat Row 4, changing to MC in last slip st.
Rows 37-39: Repeat Rows 5-7.
Row 40: With Color E, repeat Row 4, changing to Color A in last slip st.
Rows 41-43: Repeat Rows 5-7.
Rows 44-60: Repeat Rows 4-20, changing to Color D in last slip st of Row 60.
Rows 61-63: Repeat Rows 5-7.

Row 64: Repeat Row 4, changing to Color C in last slip st.
Rows 65-67: Repeat Rows 5-7.
Row 68: Repeat Row 4, changing to Color B in last slip st.
Rows 69-71: Repeat Rows 5-7.
Row 72: Repeat Row 4, changing to Color A in last slip st.

Rows 73-75: Repeat Rows 5-7.
Row 76: With Color E, repeat Row 4, changing to MC in last slip st.
Rows 77-79: Repeat Rows 5-7.
Row 80: With Color D, repeat Row 4, changing to MC in last slip st.
Rows 81-83: Repeat Rows 5-7.

Row 84: With Color C, repeat Row 4, changing to MC in last slip st.

Rows 85-87: Repeat Rows 5-7.

Row 88: With Color B, repeat Row 4, changing to MC in last slip st.

Rows 89-91: Repeat Rows 5-7.

Row 92: With Color A, repeat Row 4, changing to MC in last slip st.

Rows 93-95: Repeat Rows 5-7; at the end of Row 95, do **not** finish off.

Row 96: Turn; working in both loops, slip st in each dc across, changing to Color E in last slip st.

Rows 97-99: Repeat Rows 5-7.

Row 100: Repeat Row 4, changing to Color D in last slip st.

Rows 101-103: Repeat Rows 5-7.

Row 104: Repeat Row 4, changing to Color C in last slip st.

Rows 105-107: Repeat Rows 5-7.

Row 108: Repeat Row 4, changing to Color B in last slip st.

Rows 109-111: Repeat Rows 5-7.

Row 112: Repeat Row 4, changing to Color A in last slip st.

Rows 113-115: Repeat Rows 5-7; at the end of Row 115, do **not** finish off.

EDGING
TOP
Ch 1, turn; 2 sc in first dc, sc in next 6 dc, skip next 2 dc, sc in next 6 dc, ★ 3 sc in next dc, sc in next 6 dc, skip next 2 dc, sc in next 6 dc; repeat from ★ across to last dc, 2 sc in last dc; finish off.

BOTTOM
With **right** side facing and working in free loops of beginning ch **(Fig. 23b, page 125)**, join Color A with slip st in first ch; ch 1, pull up a loop in each of first 2 chs, YO and draw through all 3 loops on hook, sc in next 5 chs, 3 sc in next ch-2 sp, sc in next 5 chs, ★ skip next 3 chs, sc in next 5 chs, 3 sc in next ch-2 sp, sc in next 5 chs; repeat from ★ across to last 2 chs, pull up a loop in each of last 2 chs, YO and draw through all 3 loops on hook; finish off.

To make this classic comforter, panels of diamonds and cables are created simultaneously as you work across. A pretty scalloped edging adds elegance.

Finished Size: Approximately 36" x 53"

MATERIALS
Baby Sport Weight Yarn, approximately:
    30 ounces, (850 grams, 3,770 yards)
Crochet hook, size F (3.75 mm) **or** size needed for gauge

GAUGE: 15 dc and 7 rows = 3"

PATTERN STITCHES
POPCORN
5 Dc in st or sp indicated, drop loop from hook, insert hook in first dc of 5-dc group, hook dropped loop and draw through **(Fig. 16b, page 123)**.

BACK POST DOUBLE CROCHET
    (abbreviated BPdc)
YO, insert hook from **back** to **front** around post of stitch indicated, YO and pull up a loop (3 loops on hook) **(Fig. 13, page 123)**, (YO and draw through 2 loops on hook) twice.

FRONT POST DOUBLE CROCHET
    (abbreviated FPdc)
YO, insert hook from **front** to **back** around post of stitch indicated, YO and pull up a loop (3 loops on hook) **(Fig. 12, page 123)**, (YO and draw through 2 loops on hook) twice.

B4 TWIST
Skip next 2 sts, work FPtr around next 2 sts *(Fig. 1a)*; working **behind** sts just worked, dc in 2 skipped sts *(Fig. 1b)*.

Fig. 1a

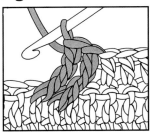

Fig. 1b

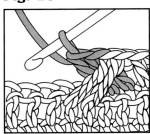

F4 TWIST
Skip next 2 sts, dc in next 2 sts *(Fig. 2a)*; working in **front** of sts just worked, work FPtr around 2 skipped sts *(Fig. 2b)*.

Fig. 2a

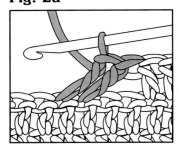

Fig. 2b

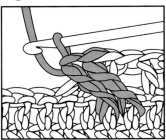

B6 CABLE
Skip next 3 sts, work FPtr around next 3 sts *(Fig. 3a)*; working **behind** sts just worked, work FPtr around 3 skipped sts *(Fig. 3b)*.

Fig. 3a

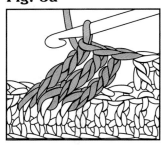

Fig. 3b

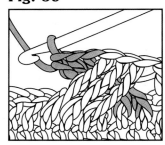

F4 CABLE
Skip next 2 sts, work FPtr around next 2 sts *(Fig. 4a)*; working in **front** of sts just worked, work FPtr around 2 skipped sts *(Fig. 4b)*.

Fig. 4a

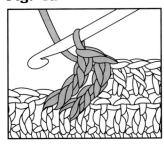

Fig. 4b

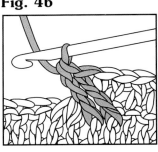

F6 CABLE
Skip next 3 sts, work FPtr around next 3 sts *(Fig. 5a)*; working in **front** of sts just worked, work FPtr around 3 skipped sts *(Fig. 5b)*.

Fig. 5a

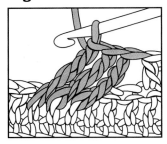

Fig. 5b

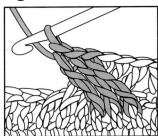

CABLE PANEL (21 sts)
Note: Panel should be 3½" wide.
Row 1 (Right side): Work BPdc around next 2 sts, work F6 Cable, work BPdc around next 2 sts, work Popcorn in next st, work BPdc around next 2 sts, work B6 Cable, work BPdc around next 2 sts.
Row 2: Work FPdc around next 2 sts, work BPdc around next 6 sts, work FPdc around next 2 sts, ch 1, skip next Popcorn, work FPdc around next 2 sts, work BPdc around next 6 sts, work FPdc around next 2 sts.
Row 3: Work BPdc around next 2 sts, work FPdc around next 6 sts, work BPdc around next 2 sts, work Popcorn in next ch-1 sp, work BPdc around next 2 sts, work FPdc around next 6 sts, work BPdc around next 2 sts.
Row 4: Repeat Row 2.
Repeat Rows 1-4 for pattern.

DIAMOND PANEL (20 sts)

Note: Panel should be 4" wide.

Row 1 (Right side): Dc in next 8 dc, work F4 Cable, dc in next 8 dc.

Row 2: Dc in next 8 dc, work BPdc around next 4 sts, dc in next 8 dc.

Row 3: Dc in next 6 dc, work B4 Twist, work F4 Twist, dc in next 6 dc.

Row 4: Dc in next 6 dc, work BPdc around next 2 sts, dc in next 4 dc, work BPdc around next 2 sts, dc in next 6 dc.

Row 5: Dc in next 4 dc, work B4 Twist, dc in next 4 dc, work F4 Twist, dc in next 4 dc.

Row 6: Dc in next 4 dc, work BPdc around next 2 sts, dc in next 8 dc, work BPdc around next 2 sts, dc in next 4 dc.

Row 7: Dc in next 2 dc, work B4 Twist, dc in next 8 dc, work F4 Twist, dc in next 2 dc.

Row 8: Dc in next 2 dc, work BPdc around next 2 sts, dc in next 12 dc, work BPdc around next 2 sts, dc in next 2 dc.

Row 9: Dc in next 2 dc, work FPdc around next 2 sts, dc in next 12 dc, work FPdc around next 2 sts, dc in next 2 dc.

Row 10: Dc in next 2 dc, work BPdc around next 2 sts, dc in next 12 dc, work BPdc around next 2 sts, dc in next 2 dc.

Row 11: Dc in next 2 dc, work F4 Twist, dc in next 8 dc, work B4 Twist, dc in next 2 dc.

Row 12: Dc in next 4 dc, work BPdc around next 2 sts, dc in next 8 dc, work BPdc around next 2 sts, dc in next 4 dc.

Row 13: Dc in next 4 dc, work F4 Twist, dc in next 4 dc, work B4 Twist, dc in next 4 dc.

Row 14: Dc in next 6 dc, work BPdc around next 2 sts, dc in next 4 dc, work BPdc around next 2 sts, dc in next 6 dc.

Row 15: Dc in next 6 dc, work F4 Twist, work B4 Twist, dc in next 6 dc.

Row 16: Dc in next 8 dc, work BPdc around next 4 sts, dc in next 8 dc.

Repeat Rows 1-16 for pattern.

BODY

Ch 188 **loosely**.

Row 1 (Right side): Sc in second ch from hook and in each ch across: 187 sc.

Row 2: Ch 3, turn; dc in next sc and in each sc across.

Row 3: Ch 3, turn; work Row 1 of Cable Panel, ★ work Row 1 of Diamond Panel, work Row 1 of Cable Panel; repeat from ★ 3 times **more**, work FPdc around turning ch.

Row 4: Ch 3, turn; work next row of Cable Panel, ★ work next row of Diamond Panel, work next row of Cable Panel; repeat from ★ 3 times **more**, work FPdc around turning ch.

Repeat Row 4 until Afghan measures approximately 51" from beginning chain, ending by working Row 1 of Diamond Panel.

Last Row: Ch 3, turn; dc in next st and in each st across; do **not** finish off.

EDGING

Rnd 1: Ch 1, turn; 3 sc in first dc, skip next dc, sc in each dc across to last st, 3 sc in last st; work 286 sc evenly spaced across end of rows to beginning ch; working in free loops of beginning ch *(Fig. 23b, page 125)*, 3 sc in first ch, skip next ch, sc in each ch across to last ch, 3 sc in last ch; work 286 sc evenly spaced across end of rows; join with slip st to first sc: 952 sc.

Rnd 2: Do **not** turn; slip st in next sc, ch 1, sc in same st, ch 5, skip next sc, sc in next sc, (ch 5, skip next 2 sc, sc in next sc) 61 times, (ch 5, skip next sc, sc in next sc) twice, (ch 5, skip next 2 sc, sc in next sc) 95 times, (ch 5, skip next sc, sc in next sc) twice, (ch 5, skip next 2 sc, sc in next sc) 61 times, (ch 5, skip next sc, sc in next sc) twice, (ch 5, skip next 2 sc, sc in next sc) 95 times, ch 5, skip last sc; join with slip st to first sc: 320 loops.

Rnd 3: Ch 1, sc in same st, ★ 7 dc in next loop, (sc in next loop, 7 dc in next loop) across to next corner sc, sc in corner sc; repeat from ★ 2 times **more**, 7 dc in next loop, (sc in next loop, 7 dc in next loop) across; join with slip st to first sc, finish off.

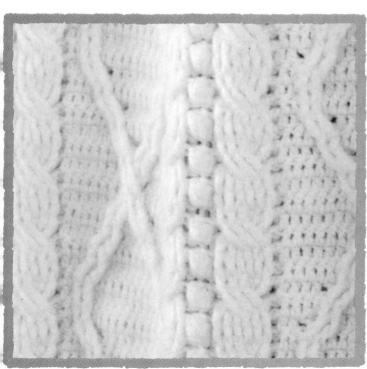

flower garland

This precious afghan offers a sweet way to shower a young miss with flowers.
Worked in sport weight yarn, the dainty motifs are joined as you go.

Finished Size: Approximately 38" x 43"

MATERIALS
Sport Weight Yarn, approximately:
 MC (White) - 8 ounces, (230 grams, 800 yards)
 Color A (Lavender) - 2 ounces,
  (60 grams, 200 yards)
 Color B (Yellow) - 3 ounces,
  (90 grams, 300 yards)
 Color C (Pink) - 2 ounces, (60 grams, 200 yards)
 Crochet hook, size D (3.25 mm) **or** size needed
  for gauge

GAUGE: Each Motif = 2¼" (side to side)

Following Placement Chart, begin with left Motif of
Row 1, and work across joining Motifs. Letter shown
in each Motif in Placement Chart indicates color used
for Rnd 1.

FIRST MOTIF
Ch 6; join with slip st to form a ring.
Rnd 1 (Right side)**:** Ch 2, (YO, insert hook in ring,
YO and pull up a loop, YO and draw through 2 loops
on hook) twice, YO and draw through all 3 loops on
hook, ch 4, ★ (YO, insert hook in ring, YO and pull
up a loop, YO and draw through 2 loops on hook) 3
times, YO and draw through all 4 loops on hook,
ch 4; repeat from ★ 4 times **more**; join with slip st to
top of first st, finish off: 6 ch-4 sps.
Note: Loop a short piece of yarn around any stitch to
mark last round as **right** side.
Rnd 2: With **right** side facing, join MC with slip st in
any ch-4 sp; ch 3, (2 dc, ch 2, 3 dc) in same sp, ch 1,
★ (3 dc, ch 2, 3 dc) in next ch-4 sp, ch 1; repeat from
★ around; join with slip st to top of beginning ch-3,
finish off: 12 sps.

PLACEMENT CHART

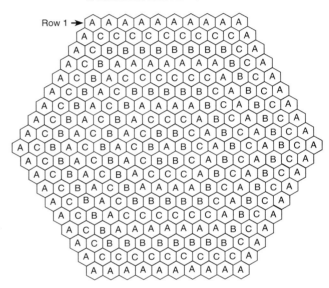

Row 1 →

ADDITIONAL MOTIFS
Ch 6; join with slip st to form a ring.
Rnd 1: Work same as First Motif.
Rnd 2: Work One, Two, or Three Side Joining
(Fig. 24, page 125).

ONE SIDE JOINING
With **right** side facing, join MC with slip st in any ch-4
sp; ch 3, 2 dc in same sp, ch 1, ★ (3 dc, ch 2, 3 dc) in
next ch-4 sp, ch 1; repeat from ★ 3 times **more**, 3 dc
in next ch-4 sp, ch 1, holding Motifs with **wrong** sides
together, slip st in ch-2 sp on **previous Motif**, ch 1,
3 dc in same ch-4 sp on **new Motif**, ch 1, slip st in
next ch-1 sp on **previous Motif**, 3 dc in same ch-4
sp as beginning ch-3 on **new Motif**, ch 1, slip st in
next ch-2 sp on **previous Motif**, ch 1; join with slip
st to top of beginning ch-3, finish off.

TWO SIDE JOINING

With **right** side facing, join MC with slip st in any ch-4 sp; ch 3, 2 dc in same sp, ch 1, ★ (3 dc, ch 2, 3 dc) in next ch-4 sp, ch 1; repeat from ★ 2 times **more**, 3 dc in next ch-4 sp, ch 1, holding Motifs with **wrong** sides together, slip st in ch-2 sp on **previous Motif**, ch 1, 3 dc in same ch-4 sp on **new Motif**, ch 1, slip st in next ch-1 sp on **previous Motif**, 3 dc in next ch-4 sp on **new Motif**, ch 1, slip st in next ch-2 sp on **previous Motif**, ch 1, slip st in next ch-2 sp on **next motif**, ch 1, 3 dc in same ch-4 sp on **new Motif**, ch 1, slip st in next ch-1 sp on **previous Motif**, 3 dc in same ch-2 sp as beginning ch-3 on **new Motif**, ch 1, slip st in next ch-2 sp on **previous Motif**, ch 1; join with slip st to top of beginning ch-3, finish off.

THREE SIDE JOINING

With **right** side facing, join MC with slip st in any ch-4 sp; ch 3, 2 dc in same sp, ch 1, **[**(3 dc, ch 2, 3 dc) in next ch-4 sp, ch 1**]** twice, 3 dc in next ch-4 sp, ch 1, holding Motifs with **wrong** sides together, slip st in

ch-2 sp on **previous Motif**, ch 1, 3 dc in same ch-4 sp on **new Motif**, ch 1, slip st in next ch-1 sp on **previous Motif**, ★ 3 dc in next ch-4 sp on **new Motif**, ch 1, slip st in next ch-2 sp on **previous Motif**, ch 1, slip st in next ch-2 sp on **next motif**, 3 dc in same ch-4 sp on **new Motif**, ch 1, slip st in next ch-1 sp on **previous Motif**; repeat from ★ once **more**, 3 dc in same ch-4 sp as beginning ch-3 on **new Motif**, ch 1, slip st in next ch-2 sp on **previous Motif**, ch 1; join with slip st to top of beginning ch-3, finish off.

EDGING

To work **decrease**, insert hook in next ch, YO and pull up a loop, skip joining, insert hook in next ch, YO and pull up a loop, YO and draw through all 3 loops on hook.

With **right** side facing, join MC with slip st in first ch of any ch-2 sp; ch 1, sc in each ch and in each dc around decreasing at each joining; join with slip st to first sc, finish off.

lullaby shells

Fanciful shells and picots accent this wrap for a little boy.
A scalloped edging complements the shell pattern.

Finished Size: Approximately 37" x 48"

MATERIALS
Worsted Weight Yarn, approximately:
22 ounces, (620 grams, 1,445 yards)
Crochet hook, size G (4.00 mm) **or** size needed
for gauge

GAUGE: In pattern, (7-dc group, Picot) twice and
8 rows = 4"

BODY
Ch 163 **loosely**.

Row 1 (Right side)**:** Sc in second ch from hook, skip
next 3 chs, 7 dc in next ch, skip next 3 chs, sc in next
ch, ★ ch 3, sc in next ch, skip next 3 chs, 7 dc in next
ch, skip next 3 chs, sc in next ch; repeat from ★
across: 18 7-dc groups.

Note: Loop a short piece of yarn around any stitch
to mark last row as **right** side.

To work **Picot**, (sc, ch 3, sc) in dc indicated.

Row 2: Ch 7 **(counts as first tr plus ch 3, now
and throughout)**, turn; work Picot in center dc of
next 7-dc group, ch 3, ★ dc in next ch-3 sp, ch 3,
work Picot in center dc of next 7-dc group, ch 3;
repeat from ★ across to last sc, tr in last sc.

Row 3: Ch 1, turn; sc in first tr, 7 dc in next Picot
(ch-3 sp), ★ work Picot in next dc, 7 dc in next
Picot; repeat from ★ across to last tr, sc in last tr.

Row 4: Ch 7, turn; work Picot in center dc of next
7-dc group, ch 3, ★ dc in next Picot, ch 3, work
Picot in center dc of next 7-dc group, ch 3; repeat
from ★ across to last sc, tr in last sc.

Repeat Rows 3 and 4 until Afghan measures
approximately 47" from beginning ch, ending by
working Row 3.

Last Row: Ch 7, turn; sc in center dc of next 7-dc
group, ch 3, ★ dc in next Picot, ch 3, sc in center dc
of next 7-dc group, ch 3; repeat from ★ across to
last sc, tr in last sc; do **not** finish off.

EDGING
Rnd 1: Ch 1, turn; 2 sc in first tr, work 147 sc
evenly spaced across to last tr, 3 sc in last tr; work
199 sc evenly spaced across end of rows; working in
free loops of beginning ch *(Fig. 23b, page 125)*,
3 sc in first ch, work 147 sc evenly spaced across to
last ch, 3 sc in last ch; work 199 sc evenly spaced
across end of rows, sc in same st as first sc; join with
slip st to first sc: 704 sc.

Rnd 2: Ch 3, do **not** turn; 4 dc in same st,
★ † skip next 2 sc, slip st in next sc, (skip next sc,
3 dc in next sc, skip next sc, slip st in next sc) across
to within 2 sc of next corner sc, skip next 2 sc †,
5 dc in corner sc; repeat from ★ 2 times **more**, then
repeat from † to † once; join with slip st to top of
beginning ch-3, finish off.

honeycomb wrap

When your busy little bee settles down for a nap, reach for our soft honeycomb wrap. Crocheted using baby sport weight yarn, the afghan features motifs in a rainbow of hushed colors.

Finished Size: Approximately 47" x 53"

MATERIALS

Baby Sport Weight Yarn, approximately:
  White - 10 ounces, (280 grams, 1,090 yards)
  Yellow - 1 ounce, (30 grams, 110 yards)
  Orange - 2 ounces, (60 grams, 220 yards)
  Pink - 2 ounces, (60 grams, 220 yards)
  Lilac - 3 ounces, (90 grams, 325 yards)
  Blue - 4 ounces, (110 grams, 435 yards)
  Green - 4 ounces, (110 grams, 435 yards)
Crochet hook size G (4.00 mm) **or** size needed for gauge
Yarn needle

GAUGE: Each Motif = 3½ " (side to side)

MOTIF #1

(Make 43 White)
Ch 4; join with slip st to form a ring.
Rnd 1 (Right side)**:** Ch 3 **(counts as first dc, now and throughout)**, dc in ring, ch 1, (2 dc in ring, ch 1) 5 times; join with slip st to first dc: 12 dc.
Note: Loop a short piece of yarn around any stitch to mark last round as **right** side.
Rnd 2: Slip st in next dc and in first ch-1 sp, ch 3, (dc, ch 1, 2 dc) in same sp, ch 1, (2 dc, ch 1) twice in next ch-1 sp and in each ch-1 sp around; join with slip st to first dc: 24 dc.
Rnd 3: Slip st in next dc and in first ch-1 sp, ch 3, (dc, ch 1, 2 dc) in same sp (corner), ch 1, dc in next ch-1 sp, ch 1, ★ (2 dc, ch 1) twice in next ch-1 sp, dc in next ch-1 sp, ch 1; repeat from ★ around; join with slip st to first dc: 30 dc.
Rnd 4: Slip st in next dc and in first ch-1 sp, ch 3, (dc, ch 1, 2 dc) in same sp, ch 1, (dc in next ch-1 sp, ch 1) twice, ★ (2 dc, ch 1) twice in next ch-1 sp, (dc in next ch-1 sp, ch 1) twice; repeat from ★ around; join with slip st to first dc: 36 dc.

Rnd 5: Slip st in next dc and in first ch-1 sp, ch 3, (dc, ch 1, 2 dc) in same sp, ch 1, (dc in next ch-1 sp, ch 1) 3 times, ★ (2 dc, ch 1) twice in next ch-1 sp, (dc in next ch-1 sp, ch 1) 3 times; repeat from ★ around; join with slip st to first dc, finish off.

MOTIF #2

(Make 6 Yellow)
Work same as Motif #1 through Rnd 4.
Rnd 5: Slip st in next dc and in first ch-1 sp, ch 3, dc in same sp, ch 1, (dc in next ch-1 sp, ch 1) 3 times, † (2 dc, ch 1) twice in next ch-1 sp, (dc in next ch-1 sp, ch 1) 3 times †, repeat from † to † once **more**, 2 dc in next ch-1 sp, cut yarn; with White, ch 1, 2 dc in same sp, ch 1, (dc in next ch-1 sp, ch 1) 3 times, repeat from † to † twice, 2 dc in same ch-1 sp as first dc, ch 1; join with slip st to first dc, finish off.

MOTIF #3

(Make 6 Orange, 12 Pink, 18 Lilac, 24 Blue, and 30 Green)
Work same as Motif #1 through Rnd 4.
Rnd 5: Slip st in next dc and in first ch-1 sp, ch 3, dc in same sp, † ch 1, (dc in next ch-1 sp, ch 1) 3 times, 2 dc in next ch-1 sp, drop yarn; with White, ch 1, 2 dc in same sp, ch 1, (dc in next ch-1 sp, ch 1) 3 times, (2 dc, ch 1) twice in next ch-1 sp, (dc in next ch-1 sp, ch 1) 3 times †, 2 dc in next ch-1 sp, drop White; with previous color, ch 1, 2 dc in same sp, repeat from † to † once, 2 dc in same ch-1 sp as first dc, ch 1; join with slip st to first dc, finish off.

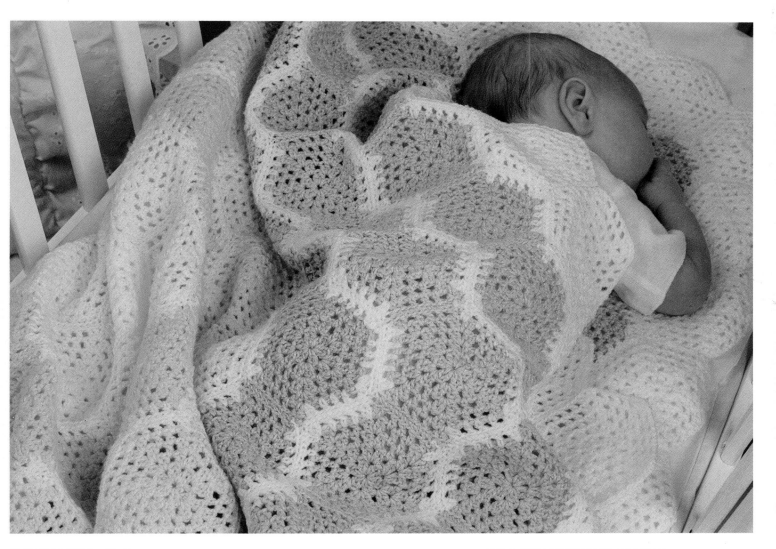

MOTIF #4

(Make 6 **each** of Orange, Pink, Lilac, Blue, and Green)

Work same as Motif #1 through Rnd 4, page 86.

Rnd 5: Slip st in next dc and in first ch-1 sp, ch 3, dc in same sp, † ch 1, (dc in next ch-1 sp, ch 1) 3 times, 2 dc in next ch-1 sp, drop yarn; with White, ch 1, 2 dc in same sp, ch 1, (dc in next ch-1 sp, ch 1) 3 times †, 2 dc in next ch-1 sp, drop White; with previous color, ch 1, 2 dc in same sp, repeat from † to † once, ★ (2 dc, ch 1) twice in next ch-1 sp, (dc in next ch-1 sp, ch 1) 3 times; repeat from ★ once **more**, 2 dc in same ch-1 sp as first dc, ch 1; join with slip st to first dc, finish off.

ASSEMBLY

With **wrong** sides together and matching color, and working through **inside** loops only, whipstitch Motifs together following Placement Diagram *(Fig. 25b, page 126)*.

PLACEMENT DIAGRAM

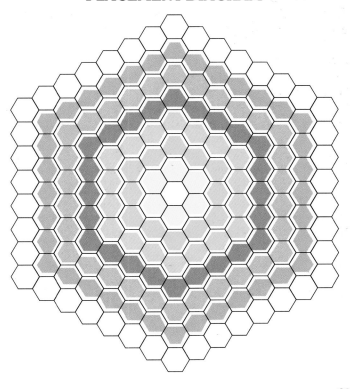

fenced·in daisy

Capturing the freshness of a spring day, our daisy motif afghan is a cheery delight. The worsted weight motifs are super easy to assemble and whipstitch together. Generous fringe enhances the "picket-fence" look.

Finished Size: Approximately 41" x 47"

MATERIALS
Worsted Weight Yarn, approximately:
  Color A (White) - 18 ounces,
    (510 grams, 1,185 yards)
  Color B (Yellow) - 6 ounces,
    (170 grams, 395 yards)
  Color C (Green) - 8 ounces,
    (230 grams, 525 yards)
Crochet hook, size H (5.00 mm) **or** size needed for
  gauge
Yarn needle

GAUGE: Each Square = 6³/₄"

SQUARE (Make 42)

Rnd 1 (Right side)**:** With Color B, ch 5, (3 dc, ch 1) 3 times in fifth ch from hook, 2 dc in same ch; join with slip st to fourth ch of beginning ch-5, finish off: 16 sts. *Note:* Loop a short piece of yarn around any stitch to mark last round as **right** side.

Rnd 2: With **right** side facing and working in Front Loops Only *(Fig. 22, page 125)*, join Color A with slip st in any ch; ★ (ch 3, 3 dc, ch 3, slip st) in same st, slip st in next 2 sts; repeat from ★ around working last slip st in first ch; finish off: 8 Petals.

Rnd 3: With **right** side facing and working in free loops of Rnd 1 (behind Petals) *(Fig. 23a, page 125)*, join Color C with slip st in any ch; ch 3 **(counts as first dc, now and throughout)**, 4 dc in same st, ch 3, skip next Petal, (5 dc in next ch, ch 3, skip next Petal) around; join with slip st to first dc: 4 5-dc groups.

Rnd 4: Slip st in next 2 dc, ch 6, dc in same st, ch 2, 3 dc in center ch of next ch-3, ch 2, ★ (dc, ch 3, dc) in center dc of next 5-dc group, ch 2, 3 dc in center ch of next ch-3, ch 2; repeat from ★ around; join with slip st to third ch of beginning ch-6.

Rnd 5: Slip st in first ch-3 sp, ch 3, (dc, ch 1, 2 dc) in same sp, ch 1, (3 dc in next ch-2 sp, ch 1) twice, ★ (2 dc, ch 1, 2 dc) in next corner ch-3 sp, ch 1, (3 dc in next ch-2 sp, ch 1) twice; repeat from ★ around; join with slip st to first dc, finish off: 40 dc.

Rnd 6: With **right** side facing, join Color A with slip st in any corner ch-1 sp; ch 3, (dc, ch 1, 2 dc) in same sp, ★ dc in each dc and in each ch across to next corner ch-1 sp, (2 dc, ch 1, 2 dc) in ch-1 sp; repeat from ★ 2 times **more**, dc in each dc and in each ch across; join with slip st to first dc: 68 dc.

Rnd 7: Ch 3, dc in next dc, (2 dc, ch 1, 2 dc) in next ch-1 sp, ★ dc in each dc across to next corner ch-1 sp, (2 dc, ch 1, 2 dc) in ch-1 sp; repeat from ★ 2 times **more**, dc in each dc across; join with slip st to first dc, finish off: 84 dc.

To work **Front Post Double Crochet** *(abbreviated FPdc)*, YO, insert hook from **front** to **back** around post of stitch indicated, YO and pull up a loop (3 loops on hook), (YO and draw through 2 loops on hook) twice *(Fig. 12, page 123)*.

Rnd 8: With **right** side facing, join Color B with sc in any corner ch-1 sp *(see Joining with Sc, page 125)*; ch 1, sc in same sp, sc in Back Loop Only of next dc, (work FPdc around next dc, sc in Back Loop Only of next dc) 10 times, ★ (sc, ch 1, sc) in next ch-1 sp, sc in Back Loop Only of next dc, (work FPdc around next dc, sc in Back Loop Only of next dc) 10 times; repeat from ★ around; join with slip st to first sc, finish off.

ASSEMBLY

With **wrong** sides together and Color B, and working through **inside** loops only, whipstitch Squares together forming 6 vertical strips of 7 Squares each; then whipstitch strips together *(Fig. 25b, page 126)*.

FRINGE

Using 4, 11" strands of Color A, add fringe in every third stitch across each end of Afghan *(Figs. 26a & b, page 126)*.

On this fanciful wrap, stripes of pink and white are bordered by layers of flirty ruffles. Satin ribbon is woven through the center picot ruffle for a feminine touch.

Finished Size: Approximately 35" x 43"

MATERIALS
Sport Weight Yarn, approximately:
  MC (Pink) - 14 ounces, (400 grams, 1,320 yards)
  CC (White) - 10½ ounces,
    (300 grams, 990 yards)
Crochet hook, size H (5.00 mm) **or** size needed
  for gauge
6½ yards of ¼" wide ribbon
Yarn needle

GAUGE: In pattern, 16 sts and 14 rows = 4"

CENTER
Note: Each row is worked across length of Afghan.
With MC, ch 141 **loosely**.
Row 1: Sc in second ch from hook, dc in next ch, (sc in next ch, dc in next ch) across: 140 sts.
Row 2 (Right side): Ch 1, turn; sc in first dc, dc in next sc, (sc in next dc, dc in next sc) across changing to CC in last dc **(Fig. 21a, page 125)**.
Note #1: Loop a short piece of yarn around any stitch to mark last row as **right** side.
Note #2: Continue to change color in the same manner.
Rows 3 and 4: With CC, ch 1, turn; sc in first dc, dc in next sc, (sc in next dc, dc in next sc) across.
Rows 5 and 6: With MC, ch 1, turn; sc in first dc, dc in next sc, (sc in next dc, dc in next sc) across.
Rows 7-94: Repeat Rows 3-6, 22 times; do **not** change color at end of Row 94.
Do **not** finish off.

EDGING
BOTTOM RUFFLE
Rnd 1: Ch 1, do **not** turn; 2 sc in top of last dc made on Row 94; work 114 sc evenly spaced across end of rows; working in free loops of beginning ch **(Fig. 23b, page 125)**, 3 sc in ch at base of first sc, sc in each ch across to last ch, 3 sc in last ch; work 114 sc evenly spaced across end of rows; 3 sc in first sc on Row 94, sc in each st across, sc in same st as first sc; join with slip st to first sc: 516 sc.
Rnd 2: Ch 4 **(counts as first hdc plus ch 2)**, hdc in same st, ch 2, † (skip next 2 sc, hdc in next sc, ch 2) 38 times, skip next 2 sc, (hdc, ch 2) twice in next sc †, (skip next 2 sc, hdc in next sc, ch 2) 46 times, skip next 2 sc, (hdc, ch 2) twice in next sc, repeat from † to † once, skip next 2 sc, (hdc in next sc, ch 2, skip next 2 sc) across; join with slip st to first hdc: 176 hdc and 176 ch-2 sps.
Rnd 3: Slip st in first ch-2 sp, ch 3 **(counts as first dc, now and throughout)**, (2 dc, ch 1, 3 dc) in same sp, ch 1, (3 dc, ch 1) twice in next ch-2 sp, † (3 dc in next ch-2 sp, ch 1) 37 times, (3 dc, ch 1) twice in each of next 3 ch-2 sps, (3 dc in next ch-2 sp, ch 1) 45 times †, (3 dc, ch 1) twice in each of next 3 ch-2 sps, repeat from † to † once, (3 dc, ch 1) twice in last ch-2 sp; join with slip st to first dc: 564 dc.
Rnd 4: Ch 3, 2 dc in next dc, (dc in next dc, 2 dc in next dc) around; join with slip st to first dc: 846 dc.
Rnds 5-8: Ch 3, dc in next dc and in each dc around; join with slip st to first dc.
To work **Picot**, ch 3, sc in third ch from hook.
Rnd 9: Ch 1, sc in same st, work Picot, skip next dc, ★ sc in next dc, work Picot, skip next dc; repeat from ★ around; join with slip st to first sc, finish off.

TOP RUFFLE

Rnd 1: With **right** side facing, holding Center toward you, and working around posts of hdc on Rnd 2 of Bottom Ruffle, join CC with sc around first hdc *(see Joining with Sc, page 125)*; ch 3, (sc around post of next hdc, ch 3) around; join with slip st to first sc: 176 ch-3 sps.

Rnd 2: Slip st in first ch-3 sp, ch 1, (sc in same sp, ch 5) 3 times, ★ (sc, ch 5) twice in next ch-3 sp, [sc in next ch-3 sp, ch 5, (sc, ch 5) twice in next ch-3 sp] across to next corner ch-3 sp, (sc, ch 5) 3 times in corner ch-3 sp; repeat from ★ 2 times **more**, [(sc, ch 5) twice in next ch-3 sp, sc in next ch-3 sp, ch 5] across to last ch-3 sp, (sc, ch 5, sc) in last ch-3 sp, ch 2, dc in first sc to form last loop: 272 loops.

Rnds 3-6: Ch 1, sc in same loop, (ch 5, sc in next loop) around, ch 2, dc in first sc to form last loop.

Rnd 7: Ch 1, (sc, work Picot, sc) in same loop, ch 3, ★ (sc, work Picot, sc) in next loop, ch 3; repeat from ★ around; join with slip st to first sc, finish off.

CENTER RUFFLE

Rnd 1: With **right** side facing, holding Bottom and Top Ruffles toward you, and working around same posts of hdc on Rnd 2 of Bottom Ruffle, join CC with sc around any hdc; ch 3, (sc around post of next hdc, ch 3) around; join with slip st to first sc: 176 ch-3 sps.

Rnd 2: Slip st in first ch-3 sp, ch 1, sc in same sp, ch 5, (sc in next ch-3 sp, ch 5) around; join with slip st to first sc.

Rnd 3: Slip st in first loop, ch 1, (sc, work Picot, sc) in same loop and in each loop around; join with slip st to first sc, finish off.

TRIM

With **right** side facing, holding Center toward you, and working around same posts of hdc on Rnd 2 of Bottom Ruffle and **between** Top and Center Ruffles, join MC with sc around any hdc; ch 3, (sc around post of next hdc, ch 3) around; join with slip st to first sc, finish off.

FINISHING

Using photo as a guide for placement, weave ribbon through Rnd 2 of Center Ruffle on each side of Afghan and tie ends in a bow at each corner.

Petite hearts created with clusters give this afghan sweet personality. The throw is constructed by whipstitching alternating heart squares and granny squares together and adding a simple border.

Finished Size: Approximately 33" x 45"

MATERIALS
Sport Weight Yarn, approximately:
   15 ounces, (430 grams, 1,415 yards)
Crochet hook, size H (5.00 mm) **or** size needed for
   gauge
Yarn needle

GAUGE: 16 sc and 18 rows = 4"
          16 dc and 9 rows = 4"
          Each Square = 6"

HEART SQUARE (Make 18)
Ch 20 **loosely**.
Row 1: Sc in second ch from hook and in each ch across: 19 sc.
Row 2 (Right side)**:** Ch 1, turn; sc in each sc across.
Note: Loop a short piece of yarn around any stitch to mark last row as **right** side.
To work **Cluster**, ★ YO, insert hook in Back Loop Only of sc indicated *(Fig. 22, page 125)*, YO and pull up a loop, YO and draw through 2 loops on hook; repeat from ★ 3 times **more**, YO and draw through all 5 loops on hook *(Figs. 14a & b, page 123)*.
Row 3: Ch 1, turn; sc in first 9 sc, work Cluster in next sc, sc in each sc across: 18 sc.
Row 4: Ch 1, turn; sc in each st across: 19 sc.
Row 5: Ch 1, turn; sc in first 7 sc, work Cluster in next sc, sc in next 3 sc, work Cluster in next sc, sc in each sc across: 17 sc.
Row 6: Ch 1, turn; sc in each st across: 19 sc.
Row 7: Ch 1, turn; sc in first 5 sc, work Cluster in next sc, sc in next 7 sc, work Cluster in next sc, sc in each sc across: 17 sc.
Row 8: Ch 1, turn; sc in each st across: 19 sc.
Row 9: Ch 1, turn; sc in first 3 sc, work Cluster in next sc, sc in next 11 sc, work Cluster in next sc, sc in each sc across: 17 sc.
Row 10: Ch 1, turn; sc in each st across: 19 sc.
Rows 11-14: Repeat Rows 9 and 10 twice.
Row 15: Ch 1, turn; sc in first 3 sc, work Cluster in next sc, (sc in next 5 sc, work Cluster in next sc) twice, sc in each sc across: 16 sc.

Row 16: Ch 1, turn; sc in each st across: 19 sc.
Row 17: Ch 1, turn; sc in first 5 sc, work Cluster in next sc, sc in next sc, work Cluster in next sc, sc in next 3 sc, work Cluster in next sc, sc in next sc, work Cluster in next sc, sc in each sc across: 15 sc.
Rows 18 and 19: Ch 1, turn; sc in each st across. Do **not** finish off.

EDGING
Rnd 1: Ch 1, turn; sc in first sc, (ch 1, skip next sc, sc in next sc) across to last 2 sc, ch 1, skip next sc, (sc, ch 2, slip st) in last sc (corner), † ch 1; working in end of rows, skip next row, slip st in next row, (ch 1, skip next row, slip st in next row) across, ch 2 †; working in free loops of beginning ch *(Fig. 23b, page 125)*, sc in first ch (corner), (ch 1, skip next ch, sc in next ch) across, ch 2, slip st in end of first row (corner); repeat from † to † once; join with slip st to first sc (corner): 40 ch-sps.
Rnd 2: Ch 1, sc in first ch-1 sp, ch 1, ★ (sc in next ch-1 sp, ch 1) across to next corner ch-2 sp, (sc, ch 2, sc) in corner ch-2 sp, ch 1; repeat from ★ around; join with slip st to first sc: 44 ch-sps.
Rnd 3: Slip st in first ch-1 sp, ch 4, ★ (dc in next ch-1 sp, ch 1) across to next corner ch-2 sp, (dc, ch 3, dc) in corner ch-2 sp, ch 1; repeat from ★ 3 times **more**, dc in last ch-1 sp, ch 1; join with slip st to third ch of beginning ch-4, finish off: 48 ch-sps.

GRANNY SQUARE (Make 17)
Rnd 1 (Right side)**:** Ch 4, 2 dc in fourth ch from hook, (ch 3, 3 dc in same ch) 3 times; dc in top of beginning ch to form last ch-3 sp: 12 sts.
Note: Mark last round as **right** side.
Rnd 2: Ch 3 **(counts as first dc, now and throughout)**, (2 dc, ch 3, 3 dc) in same sp (corner), ch 1, ★ (3 dc, ch 3, 3 dc) in next ch-3 sp (corner), ch 1; repeat from ★ 2 times **more**; join with slip st to first dc: 24 dc.

Rnd 3: Ch 4 **(counts as first dc plus ch 1, now and throughout)**, skip next dc, dc in next dc, ch 1, (dc, ch 3, dc) in next corner ch-3 sp, ch 1, ★ dc in next dc, ch 1, skip next dc, (dc in next dc, ch 1) twice, skip next dc, dc in next dc, ch 1, (dc, ch 3, dc) in next corner ch-3 sp, ch 1; repeat from ★ 2 times **more**, dc in next dc, ch 1, skip next dc, dc in next dc, ch 1; join with slip st to first dc.

Rnd 4: Ch 4, (dc in next dc, ch 1) twice, (dc, ch 3, dc) in next corner ch-3 sp, ch 1, ★ (dc in next dc, ch 1) across to next corner ch-3 sp, (dc, ch 3, dc) in corner ch-3 sp, ch 1; repeat from ★ 2 times **more**, (dc in next dc, ch 1) across; join with slip st to first dc: 32 dc.

Rnd 5: Ch 3, dc in first ch-1 sp, ★ dc in next dc, dc in each ch-1 sp and in each dc across to next corner ch-3 sp, (2 dc, ch 3, 2 dc) in corner ch-3 sp; repeat from ★ 3 times **more**, dc in each dc and in each ch-1 sp across; join with slip st to first dc: 76 dc.

Rnd 6: Ch 4, skip next dc, ★ dc in next dc, ch 1, (skip next dc, dc in next dc, ch 1) across to next corner ch-3 sp, (dc, ch 3, dc) in corner ch-3 sp, ch 1; repeat from ★ 3 times **more**, (dc in next dc, ch 1, skip next dc) across; join with slip st to first dc, finish off: 48 ch-sps.

ASSEMBLY

With **wrong** sides together and working through **both** loops, whipstitch Squares together forming 5 vertical strips of 7 Squares each following Placement Diagram *(Fig. 25a, page 126)*; then whipstitch strips together securing seam at each joining.

PLACEMENT DIAGRAM

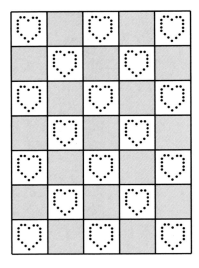

KEY

- Heart Square

- Granny Square

BORDER

Rnd 1: With **right** side facing, join yarn with sc in any corner ch-3 sp *(see Joining with Sc, page 125)*; ch 3, sc in same sp, ★ † sc in next dc, (ch 1, sc in next dc) 11 times, [ch 1, sc in joining, (ch 1, sc in next dc) 12 times] across to next corner ch-3 sp †, (sc, ch 3, sc) in corner ch-3 sp; repeat from ★ 2 times **more**, then repeat from † to † once; join with slip st to first sc: 316 sc.

Rnd 2: Slip st in first corner ch-3 sp, ch 3, (dc, ch 3, 2 dc) in same sp, ★ † ch 1, skip next sc, (dc in next sc, ch 1) across to last sc, skip last sc †, (2 dc, ch 3, 2 dc) in next corner ch-3 sp; repeat from ★ 2 times **more**, then repeat from † to † once; join with slip st to first dc: 324 dc.

Rnd 3: Slip st in next dc and in first corner ch-3 sp, ch 1, (sc, ch 3, sc) in same sp, ★ † ch 1, skip next dc, (sc in next dc, ch 1) across to within one dc of next corner ch-3 sp, skip last dc †, (sc, ch 3, sc) in corner ch-3 sp; repeat from ★ 2 times **more**, then repeat from † to † once; join with slip st to first sc.

Rnd 4: Slip st in first corner ch-3 sp, ch 3, slip st in same sp, ★ † ch 2, (slip st in next ch-1 sp, ch 2) across to next corner ch-3 sp †, (slip st, ch 3, slip st) in corner ch-3 sp; repeat from ★ 2 times **more**, then repeat from † to † once; join with slip st to first slip st, finish off.

Worked in soft yellow, floral motifs blossom against a lacy white background on our delightful afghan. A generous edging of clusters and picots borders the dainty throw.

Finished Size: Approximately 35" x 41"

MATERIALS
  Sport Weight Yarn, approximately:
    MC (White) - 13 ounces,
      (370 grams, 1,225 yards)

  CC (Yellow) - 4 ounces,
    (110 grams, 375 yards)
  Crochet hook, size F (3.75 mm) **or** size needed
    for gauge

GAUGE: Each Motif = 3¼"

PATTERN STITCHES

BEGINNING TR CLUSTER
Ch 3, ★ YO twice, insert hook in sp indicated, YO and pull up a loop, (YO and draw through 2 loops on hook) twice; repeat from ★ once **more**, YO and draw through all 3 loops on hook.

TR CLUSTER
★ YO twice, insert hook in sp indicated, YO and pull up a loop, (YO and draw through 2 loops on hook) twice; repeat from ★ 2 times **more**, YO and draw through all 4 loops on hook (*Figs. 14a & b, page 123*).

PICOT
Ch 3, sc in third ch from hook.

BEGINNING DC CLUSTER
Ch 2, ★ YO, insert hook in sp indicated, YO and pull up a loop, YO and draw through 2 loops on hook; repeat from ★ once **more**, YO and draw through all 3 loops on hook.

DC CLUSTER
★ YO, insert hook in sp indicated, YO and pull up a loop, YO and draw through 2 loops on hook; repeat from ★ 2 times **more**, YO and draw through all 4 loops on hook.

DECREASE
Pull up a loop in next 2 ch-3 sps, YO and draw through all 3 loops on hook (**counts as one sc**).

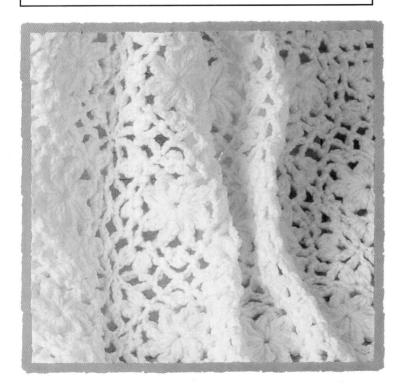

FIRST MOTIF
With CC, ch 4; join with slip st to form a ring.
Rnd 1 (Right side)**:** Work beginning tr Cluster in ring, ch 4, (work tr Cluster in ring, ch 4) 7 times; join with slip st to top of beginning tr Cluster, finish off: 8 ch-4 sps.
Note: Loop a short piece of yarn around any stitch to mark last round as **right** side.
Rnd 2: With **right** side facing, join MC with sc in any ch-4 sp (*see Joining with Sc, page 125*); ch 3, sc in same sp, ch 3, (sc, work Picot, sc) in next ch-4 sp, ch 3, ★ (sc, ch 3) twice in next ch-4 sp, (sc, work Picot, sc) in next ch-4 sp, ch 3; repeat from ★ around; join with slip st to first sc: 12 ch-3 sps and 4 Picots.
Rnd 3: Slip st in first ch-3 sp, work (beginning dc Cluster, ch 5, dc Cluster) in same sp, ch 5, sc in next ch-3 sp, ch 5, skip next Picot, sc in next ch-3 sp, ch 5, ★ (work dc Cluster, ch 5) twice in next ch-3 sp, sc in next ch-3 sp, ch 5, skip next Picot, sc in next ch-3 sp, ch 5; repeat from ★ around; join with slip st to top of beginning dc Cluster, finish off: 16 ch-5 sps.

ADDITIONAL MOTIFS
Rnds 1 and 2: Work same as First Motif: 12 ch-3 sps and 4 Picots.
Rnd 3: Work One or Two Side Joining, forming 8 rows of 10 Motifs each.

ONE SIDE JOINING
Rnd 3: Slip st in next ch and in same ch-3 sp, work beginning dc Cluster in same sp, ch 5, sc in next ch-3 sp, ch 5, skip next Picot, sc in next ch-3 sp, ch 5, ★ (work dc Cluster, ch 5) twice in next ch-3 sp, sc in next ch-3 sp, ch 5, skip next Picot, sc in next ch-3 sp, ch 5; repeat from ★ once **more**, work dc Cluster in next ch-3 sp, ch 2, holding Motifs with **wrong** sides together, sc in corner ch-5 sp on **adjacent Motif** (*Fig. 24, page 125*), ch 2, work dc Cluster in same sp on **new Motif**, ch 2, sc in next ch-5 sp on **adjacent Motif**, ch 2, sc in next ch-3 sp on **new Motif**, ch 2, sc in next ch-5 sp on **adjacent Motif**, ch 2, skip next Picot on **new Motif**, sc in next ch-3 sp, ch 2, sc in next ch-5 sp on **adjacent Motif**, ch 2, work dc Cluster in same sp as beginning dc Cluster on **new Motif**, ch 2, sc in next corner ch-5 sp on **adjacent Motif**, ch 2; join with slip st to top of beginning dc Cluster on **new Motif**, finish off.

TWO SIDE JOINING

Rnd 3: Slip st in next ch and in same ch-3 sp, work beginning dc Cluster in same sp, ch 5, sc in next ch-3 sp, ch 5, skip next Picot, sc in next ch-3 sp, ch 5, (work dc Cluster, ch 5) twice in next ch-3 sp, sc in next ch-3 sp, ch 5, skip next Picot, sc in next ch-3 sp, ch 5, work dc Cluster in next ch-3 sp, ch 2, holding Motifs with **wrong** sides together and previous Strip to your left, sc in corner ch-5 sp on **adjacent Motif**, ch 2, † work dc Cluster in same sp on **new Motif**, ch 2, sc in next ch-5 sp on **adjacent Motif**, ch 2, sc in next ch-3 sp on **new Motif**, ch 2, sc in next ch-5 sp on **adjacent Motif**, ch 2, skip next Picot on **new Motif**, sc in next ch-3 sp, ch 2, sc in next ch-5 sp on **adjacent Motif**, ch 2 †, work dc Cluster in next ch-3 sp on **new Motif**, ch 2, sc in next corner joining sc on **adjacent Motif**, ch 2, repeat from † to † once, work dc Cluster in same sp as beginning dc Cluster on **new Motif**, ch 2, sc in next corner joining sc on **adjacent Motif**, ch 2; join with slip st to top of beginning dc Cluster on **new Motif**, finish off.

EDGING

Rnd 1: With **right** side facing and working across short end, join MC with sc in right corner ch-5 sp; ch 3, sc in same sp, ch 3, (sc in next sp, ch 3) across to next corner ch-5 sp, ★ (sc, ch 3) twice in corner ch-5 sp, (sc in next sp, ch 3) across to next corner ch-5 sp; repeat from ★ around; join with slip st to first sc: 180 ch-3 sps.

Rnd 2: Slip st in first ch-3 sp, work (beginning dc Cluster, ch 3, dc Cluster) in same sp, ch 3, sc in next ch-3 sp, ch 3, ★ work (dc Cluster, ch 3) twice in next ch-3 sp, sc in next ch-3 sp, ch 3; repeat from ★ around; join with slip st to top of beginning dc Cluster: 270 ch-3 sps.

Rnd 3: Slip st in first ch-3 sp, work beginning dc Cluster in same sp, ch 3, (work dc Cluster in same sp, ch 3) twice, decrease, ch 3, ★ [(work dc Cluster, ch 3) twice in next ch-3 sp, decrease, ch 3] across to next corner ch-3 sp, (work dc Cluster, ch 3) 3 times in corner ch-3 sp, decrease, ch 3; repeat from ★ 2 times **more**, [(work dc Cluster, ch 3) twice in next ch-3 sp, decrease, ch 3] across; join with slip st to top of beginning dc Cluster: 274 ch-3 sps.

Rnd 4: Slip st in first ch-3 sp, work (beginning dc Cluster, ch 3, dc Cluster) in same sp, ch 3, (work dc Cluster, ch 3) twice in next ch-3 sp, † decrease, ch 3, [(work dc Cluster, ch 3) twice in next ch-3 sp, decrease, ch 3] 19 times, (work dc Cluster, ch 3) twice in each of next 2 ch-3 sps, decrease, ch 3, [(work dc Cluster, ch 3) twice in next ch-3 sp, decrease, ch 3] 24 times †, (work dc Cluster, ch 3) twice in each of next 2 ch-3 sps, repeat from † to † once; join with slip st to top of beginning dc Cluster: 278 ch-3 sps.

Rnd 5: Slip st in first ch-3 sp, work (beginning dc Cluster, ch 3, dc Cluster) in same sp, ch 3, (work dc Cluster, ch 3) twice in each of next 2 ch-3 sps, † decrease, ch 3, [(work dc Cluster, ch 3) twice in next ch-3 sp, decrease, ch 3] 19 times, (work dc Cluster, ch 3) twice in each of next 3 ch-3 sps, decrease, ch 3, [(work dc Cluster, ch 3) twice in next ch-3 sp, decrease, ch 3] 24 times †, (work dc Cluster, ch 3) twice in each of next 3 ch-3 sps, repeat from † to † once; join with slip st to top of beginning dc Cluster: 286 ch-3 sps.

Rnd 6: Slip st in first ch-3 sp, work (beginning dc Cluster, ch 3, dc Cluster) in same sp, ch 3, sc in next ch-3 sp, ch 3, (work dc Cluster, ch 3) 3 times in next ch-3 sp, sc in next ch-3 sp, ch 3, (work dc Cluster, ch 3) twice in next ch-3 sp, † [decrease, ch 3, (work dc Cluster, ch 3) twice in next ch-3 sp] 20 times, sc in next ch-3 sp, ch 3, (work dc Cluster, ch 3) 3 times in next ch-3 sp, sc in next ch-3 sp, ch 3, (work dc Cluster, ch 3) twice in next ch-3 sp †, [decrease, ch 3, (work dc Cluster, ch 3) twice in next ch-3 sp] 25 times, sc in next ch-3 sp, ch 3, (work dc Cluster, ch 3) 3 times in next ch-3 sp, sc in next ch-3 sp, ch 3, (work dc Cluster, ch 3) twice in next ch-3 sp, repeat from † to † once, decrease, ch 3, [(work dc Cluster, ch 3) twice in next ch-3 sp, decrease, ch 3] across; join with slip st to top of beginning dc Cluster: 298 ch-3 sps.

Rnd 7: Slip st in first ch-3 sp, work (beginning dc Cluster, ch 3, dc Cluster) in same sp, ch 3, decrease, ch 3, † (work dc Cluster, ch 3) twice in each of next 2 ch-3 sps, decrease, ch 3, [(work dc Cluster, ch 3) twice in next ch-3 sp, decrease, ch 3] 21 times, (work dc Cluster, ch 3) twice in each of next 2 ch-3 sps, decrease, ch 3 †, [(work dc Cluster, ch 3) twice in next ch-3 sp, decrease, ch 3] 26 times, repeat from † to † once, [(work dc Cluster, ch 3) twice in next ch-3 sp, decrease, ch 3] across; join with slip st to top of beginning dc Cluster: 302 ch-3 sps.

Rnd 8: Slip st in first ch-3 sp, work (beginning dc Cluster, ch 3, dc Cluster) in same sp, ch 3, decrease, ch 3, (work dc Cluster, ch 3) twice in next ch-3 sp, † sc in next ch-3 sp, ch 3, (work dc Cluster, ch 3) twice in next ch-3 sp, [decrease, ch 3, (work dc Cluster, ch 3) twice in next ch-3 sp] 22 times, sc in next ch-3 sp, ch 3 †, (work dc Cluster, ch 3) twice in next ch-3 sp, [decrease, ch 3, (work dc Cluster, ch 3) twice in next ch-3 sp] 27 times, repeat from † to † once, [(work dc Cluster, ch 3) twice in next ch-3 sp, decrease, ch 3] across; join with slip st to top of beginning dc Cluster: 306 ch-3 sps.

Rnd 9: Slip st in first ch-3 sp, work (beginning dc Cluster, Picot, dc Cluster) in same sp, ch 4, decrease, ch 4, ★ work (dc Cluster, Picot, dc Cluster) in next ch-3 sp, ch 4, decrease, ch 4; repeat from ★ around; join with slip st to top of beginning dc Cluster, finish off.

baby·soft ripples

This plush afghan of brushed acrylic yarn is created using a variety of stitches including shells, clusters, and V-stitches. Worked in lacy candy-striped ripples, the snuggly coverlet is baby soft!

Finished Size: Approximately 38" x 46"

MATERIALS
Worsted Weight Brushed Acrylic Yarn, approximately:
- MC (White) - 10 ounces,
  (280 grams, 770 yards)
- Color A (Mint) - 3 ounces,
  (90 grams, 230 yards)
- Color B (Blue) - 3 ounces,
  (90 grams, 230 yards)
- Color C (Yellow) - 3 ounces,
  (90 grams, 230 yards)
- Color D (Peach) - 3 ounces,
  (90 grams, 230 yards)
- Crochet hook, size H (5.00 mm) **or** size needed for gauge

GAUGE: 2 Repeats from point to point and 8 rows = 5"

PATTERN STITCHES
V-ST
(Dc, ch 1, dc) in st indicated.
SHELL
Dc in st indicated, (ch 1, dc in same st) twice.
CLUSTER (uses next 5 sps **and** sts)
YO, insert hook in next ch-1 sp, YO and pull up a loop, YO and draw through 2 loops on hook, ★ YO, skip next dc, insert hook in **next** st or sp, YO and pull up a loop, YO and draw through 2 loops on hook; repeat from ★ once **more**, YO and draw through all 4 loops on hook *(Figs. 15a & b, page 123)*.
ENDING CLUSTER (uses last sp and last 2 sts)
★ YO, insert hook in **next** sp or st, YO and pull up a loop, YO and draw through 2 loops on hook; repeat from ★ 2 times **more**, YO and draw through all 4 loops on hook.
DECREASE (uses next st and next ch-1 sp)
★ YO, insert hook in **next** st or sp, YO and pull up a loop, YO and draw through 2 loops on hook; repeat from ★ once **more**, YO and draw through all 3 loops on hook.

STRIPE SEQUENCE
One row of **each** color: Color A *(Fig. 21a, page 125)*, ★ MC, Color B, MC, Color C, MC, Color D, MC, Color A; repeat from ★ 8 times **more**.

BODY
With Color A, ch 182 **loosely**.

Row 1 (Right side)**:** YO, insert hook in third ch from hook, YO and pull up a loop, YO and draw through 2 loops on hook, YO, insert hook in next ch, YO and pull up a loop, YO and draw through 2 loops on hook, YO and draw through all 3 loops on hook, skip next ch, work V-St in next ch, skip next ch, work Shell in next ch, skip next ch, work V-St in next ch, ★ (YO, skip **next** ch, insert hook in **next** ch, YO and pull up a loop, YO and draw through 2 loops on hook) 3 times, YO and draw through all 4 loops on hook, skip next ch, work V-St in next ch, skip next ch, work Shell in next ch, skip next ch, work V-St in next ch; repeat from ★ across to last 4 chs, skip next ch, work ending Cluster: 105 dc.

Note: Loop a short piece of yarn around any stitch to mark last row as **right** side.

Rows 2-73: Ch 2, turn; decrease, skip next dc, work V-St in next dc, skip next ch-1 sp, work Shell in next dc, skip next ch-1 sp, work V-St in next dc, ★ skip next dc, work Cluster, skip next dc, work V-St in next dc, skip next ch-1 sp, work Shell in next dc, skip next ch-1 sp, work V-St in next dc; repeat from ★ across to last V-St, skip next dc, work ending Cluster.
Finish off.

welcome home

The eight pretty scallops at each end of this dreamy afghan are worked one at a time between the eyelet rows. Woven with soft satin ribbon, the wrap will make a beautiful "welcome home" gift for baby.

Finished Size: Approximately 33" x 44"

MATERIALS
 Baby Yarn, approximately:
  16 ounces, (450 grams, 1790 yards)
 Crochet hook, size F (3.75 mm) **or** size needed
  for gauge
 18¼ yards of ¼" wide satin ribbon
 Tapestry needle
 Sewing needle and thread to match ribbon

GAUGE: 21 dc and 10 rows = 4"

Note: Each row is worked across length of Afghan.

BODY
Ch 209 **loosely**.
Row 1 (Eyelet row)**:** Dc in eighth ch from hook,
(ch 2, skip next 2 chs, dc in next ch) across: 68 sps.
Row 2 (Right side)**:** Ch 3 **(counts as first dc, now
and throughout)**, turn; 3 dc in next ch-2 sp and in
each ch-2 sp across to last sp, 4 dc in last sp: 206 dc.
Note: Loop a short piece of yarn around any stitch to
mark last row as **right** side.
Row 3: Ch 3, turn; skip next dc, (dc, ch 1, dc) in
next dc, ★ skip next 2 dc, (dc, ch 1, dc) in next dc;
repeat from ★ across to last 2 dc, skip next dc, dc in
last dc: 68 ch-1 sps.
Row 4: Ch 3, turn; 3 dc in next ch-1 sp and in each
ch-1 sp across, dc in last dc: 206 dc.
Rows 5-10: Repeat Rows 3 and 4, 3 times.
Row 11 (Eyelet row)**:** Ch 5 **(counts as first dc plus
ch 2)**, turn; skip next 3 dc, dc in next dc, (ch 2, skip
next 2 dc, dc in next dc) across: 68 ch-2 sps.
Row 12: Ch 3, turn; 3 dc in next ch-2 sp and in
each ch-2 sp across, dc in last dc: 206 dc.
Rows 13-81: Repeat Rows 3-12, 6 times; then
repeat Rows 3-11 once **more**.
Finish off.

SCALLOPS
Note: Scallops are worked one at a time across end of
rows on each end of Afghan. Each Scallop is worked
between the ends of two Eyelet rows.

FIRST END - FIRST SCALLOP
Row 1: With **wrong** side facing, join yarn with slip st
in end of sixth row from corner (center row between
two Eyelet rows); ch 1, (sc, ch 5, sc) in same sp.
Row 2: Ch 3, slip st in end of next row, turn; 9 dc in
ch-5 sp, slip st in end of next row: 10 dc.
Row 3: Ch 3, slip st in end of next row, ch 1, turn;
skip first dc, (dc in next dc, ch 1) 8 times, dc in next
dc, slip st in end of next row.
Row 4: Ch 3, slip st in end of next row, ch 2, turn;
skip first dc, (dc in next dc, ch 2) 8 times, dc in next
dc, slip st in end of next row.
Row 5: Ch 3, slip st in end of next row, ch 2, turn;
dc in first dc, (dc, ch 2, dc) in next 9 dc, slip st in end
of next row; finish off: 20 dc.

SECOND THROUGH EIGHTH SCALLOPS
Row 1: With **wrong** side facing, skip next 5 rows
from last Scallop made and join yarn with slip st in end
of next row; ch 1, (sc, ch 5, sc) in same sp.
Row 2: Ch 3, slip st in end of next row, turn; 9 dc in
ch-5 sp, slip st in end of next row: 10 dc.
Row 3: Ch 3, slip st in end of next row, ch 1, turn;
skip first dc, (dc in next dc, ch 1) 8 times, dc in next
dc, slip st in end of next row.
Row 4: Ch 3, slip st in end of next row, ch 2, turn;
skip first dc, (dc in next dc, ch 2) 8 times, dc in next
dc, slip st in end of next row.
Row 5: Ch 3, slip st in end of next row, ch 2, turn;
dc in first dc, (dc, ch 2, dc) in next 9 dc, slip st in end
of next row; finish off: 20 dc.

SECOND END
Work same as First End; do **not** finish off at end of
Eighth Scallop.

EDGING

Turn; slip st in first dc and in next ch-2 sp, ch 1, sc in same sp, (sc, ch 3, sc) in next 8 ch-2 sps, sc in next ch-2 sp, ★ **[**sc in first ch-2 sp of next Scallop, (sc, ch 3, sc) in next 8 ch-2 sps, sc in next ch-2 sp**]** across to next corner sp, sc in corner sp, (ch 3, sc) twice in same sp, (sc, ch 3, sc) in each ch-2 sp across to next corner sp, sc in corner sp, (ch 3, sc) twice in same sp;

repeat from ★ once **more**; join with slip st to first sc, finish off.

With **right** side facing, weave ribbon through each Eyelet row; tack ribbon ends to **wrong** side of Afghan. For bows, cut fourteen 16" lengths of ribbon. Tie each length in a bow and tack to each end of Eyelet rows.

pastel waves

Alternating shells and clusters create a sea of tranquil waves on this precious wrap. A delicate white edging completes the comfy cover-up.

Finished Size: Approximately 37" x 48"

MATERIALS

Worsted Weight Yarn, approximately:
MC (White) - 14 ounces,
(400 grams, 920 yards)
Color A (Blue) - 6½ ounces,
(190 grams, 430 yards)
Color B (Pink) - 6½ ounces,
(190 grams, 430 yards)
Crochet hook, size G (4.00 mm) **or** size needed
for gauge

GAUGE: In pattern, (sc, 5-dc group) twice
and 6 rows = 3"

BODY

With MC, ch 142 **loosely**.

Row 1 (Right side)**:** 2 Dc in fourth ch from hook, skip next 2 chs, sc in next ch, ★ skip next 2 chs, 5 dc in next ch, skip next 2 chs, sc in next ch; repeat from ★ across to last 3 chs, skip next 2 chs, 3 dc in last ch changing to Color A in last dc *(Fig. 21a, page 125)*: 22 5-dc groups.

Note: Loop a short piece of yarn around any stitch to mark last row as **right** side.

To work **Cluster** (uses next 5 sts), ★ YO, insert hook in **next** st, YO and pull up a loop, YO and draw through 2 loops on hook; repeat from ★ 4 times **more**, YO and draw through all 6 loops on hook *(Figs. 15a & b, page 123)*.

Row 2: Ch 1, turn; sc in first dc, ch 2, work Cluster, ch 2, ★ sc in next dc, ch 2, work Cluster, ch 2; repeat from ★ across to last st, sc in top of beginning ch: 23 Clusters.

Row 3: Ch 3 **(counts as first dc, now and throughout)**, turn; 2 dc in same st, sc in next Cluster, ★ 5 dc in next sc, sc in next Cluster; repeat from ★ across to last sc, 3 dc in last sc changing to MC in last dc.

Row 4: Ch 1, turn; sc in first dc, ★ ch 2, work Cluster, ch 2, sc in next dc; repeat from ★ across.

Row 5: Ch 3, turn; 2 dc in same st, sc in next Cluster, ★ 5 dc in next sc, sc in next Cluster; repeat from ★ across to last sc, 3 dc in last sc changing to Color B in last dc.

Row 6: Ch 1, turn; sc in first dc, ★ ch 2, work Cluster, ch 2, sc in next dc; repeat from ★ across.

Row 7: Ch 3, turn; 2 dc in same st, sc in next Cluster, ★ 5 dc in next sc, sc in next Cluster; repeat from ★ across to last sc, 3 dc in last sc changing to MC in last dc.

Row 8: Ch 1, turn; sc in first dc, ★ ch 2, work Cluster, ch 2, sc in next dc; repeat from ★ across.

Row 9: Ch 3, turn; 2 dc in same st, sc in next Cluster, ★ 5 dc in next sc, sc in next Cluster; repeat from ★ across to last sc, 3 dc in last sc changing to Color A in last dc.

Row 10: Ch 1, turn; sc in first dc, ★ ch 2, work Cluster, ch 2, sc in next dc; repeat from ★ across.

Repeat Rows 3-10 until Afghan measures approximately 46" from beginning ch, ending by working Row 4; do **not** finish off.

EDGING

Rnd 1: Ch 1, turn; 3 sc in first sc, work 148 sc evenly spaced across to last sc, 3 sc in last sc; work 205 sc evenly spaced across end of rows; working in free loops of beginning ch *(Fig. 23b, page 125)*, 3 sc in first ch, work 148 sc evenly spaced across to last ch, 3 sc in last ch; work 205 sc evenly spaced across end of rows; join with slip st to first sc: 718 sc.

Rnd 2: Ch 1, turn; sc in same st and in each sc around working 3 sc in each corner sc; join with slip st to first sc: 726 sc.

Rnd 3: Ch 1, turn; (sc, ch 3, slip st) in same st, skip next 2 sc, ★ (sc, ch 3, slip st) in next sc, skip next 2 sc; repeat from ★ around; join with slip st to first sc, finish off.

103

petal stripes

Reminiscent of blossom-embellished Maypole ribbons, pastel stripes and three-dimensional flower petals give this afghan carefree appeal. The worsted weight throw is worked from end to end and finished with a generous fringe.

Finished Size: Approximately 32" x 45"

MATERIALS
Worsted Weight Yarn, approximately:
    MC (White) - 16 ounces,
        (450 grams, 1,055 yards)
    Color A (Green) - 4 ounces,
        (110 grams, 265 yards)
    Color B (Yellow) - 3 ounces,
        (90 grams, 200 yards)
Crochet hook, size I (5.50 mm) **or** size needed
    for gauge

GAUGE: In pattern, 13 dc and 12 rows = 4"

Note: Each row is worked across length of Afghan.

BODY
With MC, ch 149 **loosely**.

Row 1 (Right side)**:** Dc in fourth ch from hook and in each ch across: 147 sts.

Note: Loop a short piece of yarn around any stitch to mark last row as **right** side.

Row 2: Ch 1, turn; sc in first dc, (skip next st, 2 sc in next st) across: 147 sc.

Row 3: Ch 3, turn; dc in next sc and in each sc across.

Row 4: Ch 1, turn; 2 sc in first dc, (skip next dc, 2 sc in next dc) across to last 2 sts, skip next st, sc in last st; finish off: 147 sc.

To work **Small Petal**, (slip st, ch 3, 2 dc, ch 3, slip st) in next sc.

Row 5: With **right** side facing, join Color B with sc in first sc *(see Joining with Sc, page 125)*; sc in next 9 sc, work Small Petal, (sc in next 20 sc, work Small Petal) 6 times, sc in last 10 sc: 7 Small Petals.

Row 6: Ch 1, turn; sc in first 10 sc, ch 1, (skip next Small Petal, sc in next 20 sc, ch 1) 6 times, skip next Small Petal, sc in last 10 sc; finish off: 140 sc.

To work **Petal**, (slip st, ch 3, 4 tr, ch 3, slip st) in next ch-1 sp.

Row 7: With **right** side facing, join Color A with sc in first sc; sc in next 9 sc, work Petal, (sc in next 20 sc, work Petal) 6 times, sc in last 10 sc: 7 Petals.

Row 8: Ch 1, turn; sc in first 9 sc, ch 3, (skip next sc, skip next Petal and next sc, sc in next 18 sc, ch 3) 6 times, skip next sc, skip next Petal and next sc, sc in last 9 sc; finish off: 126 sc.

Row 9: With **right** side facing, join MC with slip st in first sc; ch 3, dc in next 8 sc, 3 dc in next ch-3 sp, (dc in next 18 sc, 3 dc in next ch-3 sp) 6 times, dc in last 9 sc: 147 sts.

Rows 10-12: Repeat Rows 2-4; do **not** finish off.

Row 13: Ch 3, turn; dc in next sc and in each sc across.

Rows 14-96: Repeat Rows 2-13, 6 times; then repeat Rows 2-12 once **more**.
Finish off.

FRINGE
Using 4, 11" strands of MC, add fringe in every other row across each end of Afghan *(Figs. 26c & d, page 126)*.

Reminiscent of twirling toy pinwheels, the motifs in this afghan are worked separately and then whipstitched together. The playful throw is full of eye-catching fun, even when baby is napping!

Finished Size: Approximately 37" x 49"

MATERIALS
Sport Weight Yarn, approximately:
   21 ounces, (600 grams, 1,980 yards)
Crochet hook, size F (3.75 mm) **or** size needed
   for gauge
Yarn needle

GAUGE: Each Motif = 6"

MOTIF (Make 52)
Ch 4; join with slip st to form a ring.
Rnd 1 (Right side)**:** Ch 1, (sc in ring, ch 2) 6 times; join with slip st to first sc: 6 ch-2 sps.
Note: Loop a short piece of yarn around any stitch to mark last round as **right** side.
Rnd 2: Slip st in first ch-2 sp, ch 1, sc in same sp and in next sc, ch 3, (sc in next ch-2 sp and in next sc, ch 3) 4 times, sc in last ch-2 sp and in same st as joining, ch 3; join with slip st to first sc: 12 sc and 6 ch-3 sps.
Note: Markers are used to help distinguish the beginning of each round being worked. Place a 2" scrap piece of yarn around first ch-3 of round, moving marker after each round is complete.
Rnd 3: Ch 3, skip next sc, 2 sc in next ch-3 sp, ★ sc in next sc, ch 3, 2 sc in next ch-3 sp; repeat from ★ 4 times **more**, sc in same st as joining; do **not** join, place marker: 18 sc.
Rnd 4: ★ Ch 3, 2 sc in next ch-3 sp, sc in next 2 sc; repeat from ★ around: 24 sc.
Rnd 5: ★ Ch 3, 2 sc in next ch-3 sp, sc in next 3 sc; repeat from ★ around: 30 sc.
Rnd 6: ★ Ch 3, 2 sc in next ch-3 sp, sc in next 4 sc; repeat from ★ around: 36 sc.
Rnd 7: ★ Ch 3, 2 sc in next ch-3 sp, sc in next 5 sc; repeat from ★ around: 42 sc.
Rnd 8: ★ Ch 3, 2 sc in next ch-3 sp, sc in next 6 sc; repeat from ★ around: 48 sc.
Rnd 9: ★ Ch 3, 2 sc in next ch-3 sp, sc in next 7 sc; repeat from ★ around: 54 sc.

Rnd 10: ★ Ch 3, 2 sc in next ch-3 sp, sc in next 8 sc; repeat from ★ around: 60 sc.
Rnd 11: ★ Ch 3, 2 sc in next ch-3 sp, sc in next 9 sc; repeat from ★ around: 66 sc.
Rnd 12: Ch 3, ★ 2 sc in next ch-3 sp, sc in next 10 sc, ch 3; repeat from ★ around, slip st in next sc; finish off: 72 sc.

ASSEMBLY
With **wrong** sides together, and working through **inside** loops only, whipstitch Motifs together forming 4 vertical strips of 7 Motifs each and 3 vertical strips of 8 Motifs each following Placement Diagram *(Fig. 25b, page 126)*; then whipstitch strips together.

(Fig. 25b, page 126)

PLACEMENT DIAGRAM

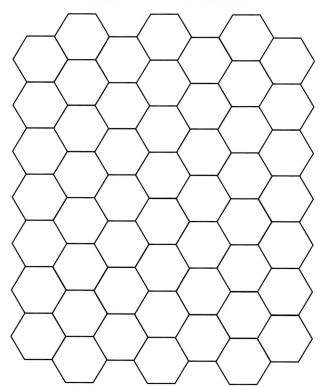

EDGING

Rnd 1: With **right** side facing, join yarn with sc in any sc *(see Joining with Sc, page 125)*; sc in each sc around working 4 sc in each ch-3 sp and 2 sc in sp at each side of joining; join with slip st to first sc.

Rnd 2: Ch 1, do **not** turn; hdc in same st, ch 1, working from **left** to **right**, skip next sc, ★ work reverse hdc in next sc *(Figs. 19a-d, page 124)*, ch 1, skip next sc; repeat from ★ around; join with slip st to first hdc, finish off.

*Crocheted using sport weight yarn, this feminine throw is
abloom with the colors of springtime. The hexagon-shaped motifs
are worked separately, then joined and edged with single crochet.*

Finished Size: Approximately 27" x 40"

MATERIALS
Sport Weight Yarn, approximately:
    MC (Pink) - 4½ ounces,
        (130 grams, 450 yards)
    Color A (White) - 5½ ounces,
        (160 grams, 550 yards)
    Color B (Green) - 1½ ounces,
        (40 grams, 150 yards)
    4 Contrasting Colors (Purple, Blue, Yellow,
        Peach) - ½ ounce, (15 grams, 50 yards) **each**
Crochet hook, size E (3.50 mm) **or** size needed for
    gauge
Yarn needle

GAUGE: Each Motif = 5½" (side to side)

PATTERN STITCHES
POPCORN
4 Dc in next sc, drop loop from hook, insert hook
in first dc of 4-dc group, hook dropped loop and
draw through *(Fig. 16a, page 123)*.
CLUSTER
(YO, insert hook in sp indicated, YO and pull up a
loop, YO and draw through 2 loops on hook) 3
times, YO and draw through all 4 loops on hook
(Figs. 14a & b, page 123).

MOTIF (Make 32)
Note: For Rnds 1 and 2, make 6 Motifs using MC,
make 6 Motifs **each** using first two Contrasting Colors,
and make 7 Motifs **each** using remaining two
Contrasting Colors.

Rnd 1 (Right side)**:** Ch 2, 6 sc in second ch from
hook; join with slip st to first sc.
Note: Loop a short piece of yarn around any stitch to
mark last round as **right** side.
Rnd 2: Ch 3 **(counts as first dc, now and
throughout)**, 3 dc in same sc, drop loop from hook,
insert hook in first dc of 4-dc group, hook dropped
loop and draw through, ch 3, (work Popcorn, ch 3)
around; join with slip st to first st, finish off: 6 ch-3
sps.
Rnd 3: With **right** side facing, join Color B with slip
st in any ch-3 sp; ch 3, (YO, insert hook in same sp,
YO and pull up a loop, YO and draw through 2 loops
on hook) twice, YO and draw through all 3 loops on
hook, ch 3, work Cluster in same sp, ch 1, ★ work
(Cluster, ch 3, Cluster) in next ch-3 sp, ch 1; repeat
from ★ around; join with slip st to first st, finish off:
12 Clusters.
Rnd 4: With **right** side facing, join Color A with slip
st in any ch-3 sp; ch 3, (2 dc, ch 2, 3 dc) in same sp,
ch 1, 3 dc in next ch-1 sp, ch 1, ★ (3 dc, ch 2, 3 dc)
in next ch-3 sp, ch 1, 3 dc in next ch-1 sp, ch 1;
repeat from ★ around; join with slip st to first dc:
54 dc.
Rnd 5: Slip st in next 2 dc and in first ch-2 sp, ch 3,
(2 dc, ch 2, 3 dc) in same sp, 3 dc in each of next
2 ch-1 sps, ★ (3 dc, ch 2, 3 dc) in next ch-2 sp, 3 dc
in each of next 2 ch-1 sps; repeat from ★ around; join
with slip st to first dc, finish off: 72 dc.
Rnd 6: With **right** side facing, join MC with slip st in
any ch-2 sp; ch 3, dc in same sp, dc in each dc across
to next ch-2 sp, ★ 2 dc in next ch-2 sp, dc in each dc
across to next ch-2 sp; repeat from ★ around; join
with slip st to first dc, finish off: 84 dc.

ASSEMBLY

Using Placement Diagram as a guide, join 6 Motifs into 3 vertical strips and 7 Motifs into 2 vertical strips. Join Motifs as follows:

With **wrong** sides together and working through inside loops only **(Fig. 25b, page 126)**, join MC with slip st in second dc of any 2-dc group; slip st in each dc across to next 2-dc group, slip st in next dc; finish off. Join strips together in same manner.

PLACEMENT DIAGRAM

EDGING

Rnd 1: With **right** side facing, join MC with slip st in second dc of 2-dc group at Point A **(see Diagram)**; ch 1, 2 sc in same st, † sc in next 26 dc, 2 sc in next 2 dc, sc in next 12 dc, 2 sc in next 2 dc, sc in next 40 dc, 2 sc in next 2 dc, sc in next 12 dc, 2 sc in next 2 dc, sc in next 26 dc, 2 sc in next 2 dc, sc in next 12 dc, 2 sc in next 2 dc, (sc in next 26 dc, 2 sc in next 2 dc) 5 times, sc in next 12 dc †, 2 sc in next 2 dc, repeat from † to † once, 2 sc in last dc; join with slip st to first sc.

Rnd 2: Ch 1, 2 sc in first sc, † sc in next 13 sc, skip next 2 sc, sc in next 13 sc, 2 sc in next 2 sc, sc in next 14 sc, 2 sc in next 2 sc, sc in next 13 sc, skip next 2 sc, sc in next 12 sc, skip next 2 sc, sc in next 13 sc, 2 sc in next 2 sc, sc in next 14 sc, 2 sc in next 2 sc, sc in next 13 sc, skip next 2 sc, sc in next 13 sc, 2 sc in next 2 sc, sc in next 14 sc, 2 sc in next 2 sc, (sc in next 13 sc, skip next 2 sc, sc in next 13 sc, 2 sc in next 2 sc) 5 times, sc in next 14 sc †, 2 sc in next 2 sc, repeat from † to † once, 2 sc in last sc; join with slip st to first sc.

Rnd 3: Ch 1, 2 sc in first sc, † sc in next 13 sc, skip next 2 sc, sc in next 13 sc, 2 sc in next 2 sc, sc in next 16 sc, 2 sc in next 2 sc, sc in next 13 sc, skip next 2 sc, sc in next 10 sc, skip next 2 sc, sc in next 13 sc, 2 sc in next 2 sc, sc in next 16 sc, 2 sc in next 2 sc, sc in next 13 sc, skip next 2 sc, sc in next 13 sc, 2 sc in next 2 sc, sc in next 16 sc, 2 sc in next 2 sc, (sc in next 13 sc, skip next 2 sc, sc in next 13 sc, 2 sc in next 2 sc) 5 times, sc in next 16 sc †, 2 sc in next 2 sc, repeat from † to † once, 2 sc in last sc; join with slip st to first sc, finish off.

Lacy V-stitches and double crochets create alternating panels of texture on our rock-a-bye blanket. Variegated yarn in white, pink, and blue makes this pastel afghan nice for boys or girls.

Finished Size: Approximately 36" x 45"

MATERIALS

Worsted Weight Yarn, approximately:
MC (Variegated) - 16 ounces,
  (450 grams, 1,055 yards)
CC (White) - 5 ounces, (140 grams, 330 yards)
Crochet hook, size G (4.00 mm) **or** size needed for gauge

GAUGE: 21 dc and 10 rows = 5¼"

STRIPE SEQUENCE

Work 5 rows MC, ★ 1 row CC, 3 rows MC, 1 row CC, 5 rows MC; repeat from ★ throughout **(Fig. 21a, page 125)**.

BODY

With MC, ch 148 **loosely**.

Row 1 (Right side)**:** 3 Dc in fifth ch from hook, (skip next 2 chs, 3 dc in next ch) across to last 2 chs, skip next ch, dc in last ch: 146 sts.

Note: Loop a short piece of yarn around any stitch to mark last row as **right** side.

Row 2: Ch 3 **(counts as first dc, now and throughout)**, turn; skip next dc, 3 dc in next dc, (skip next 2 dc, 3 dc in next dc) across to last 2 sts, skip last dc, dc in top of beginning ch: 146 dc.

Rows 3-5: Ch 3, turn; skip next dc, 3 dc in next dc, (skip next 2 dc, 3 dc in next dc) across to last 2 dc, skip next dc, dc in last dc.

Row 6: Ch 3, turn; dc in next dc and in each dc across.

To work **V-St**, (dc, ch 1, dc) in st or sp indicated.

Row 7: Ch 3, turn; skip next dc, work V-St in next dc, (skip next 2 dc, work V-St in next dc) across to last 2 dc, skip next dc, dc in last dc: 48 ch-1 sps.

Rows 8 and 9: Ch 3, turn; work V-St in each ch-1 sp across to last 2 dc, skip next dc, dc in last dc.

Row 10: Ch 3, turn; dc in next dc and in each ch-1 sp and each dc across: 146 dc.

Rows 11-15: Ch 3, turn; skip next dc, 3 dc in next dc, (skip next 2 dc, 3 dc in next dc) across to last 2 dc, skip next dc, dc in last dc.

Rows 16-85: Repeat Rows 6-15, 7 times. Finish off.

EDGING

With **right** side facing, join CC with slip st in any st; ch 3, dc evenly around working 3 dc in each corner; join with slip st to first dc, finish off.

soft and wonderful

Blue and white worsted weight yarns combine to make this breezy blanket. The small, square afghan features "windowpanes" of double crochet stitches anchored in rounds of chain loops and single crochets. A picot edging adds a flirty finish.

Finished Size: Approximately 33" x 33"

MATERIALS

Worsted Weight Yarn, approximately:
  MC (Blue) - 9 ounces, (260 grams, 570 yards)
  CC (White) - 6 ounces, (170 grams, 380 yards)
Crochet hook, size I (5.50 mm) **or** size needed for gauge

GAUGE: Rnds 1-5 = 6"

With MC, ch 5; join with slip st to form a ring.
Rnd 1 (Right side)**:** Ch 3 **(counts as first dc, now and throughout)**, 2 dc in ring, ch 1, (3 dc in ring, ch 1) 3 times; join with slip st to first dc, finish off: 12 dc.
Note: Loop a short piece of yarn around any stitch to mark last round as **right** side.

Rnd 2: With **right** side facing, join CC with sc in any ch-1 sp *(see Joining with Sc, page 125)*; ch 3, sc in same sp, ch 3, (sc, ch 3) twice in each ch-1 sp around; join with slip st to first sc, finish off: 8 ch-3 sps.
Rnd 3: With **right** side facing, join MC with slip st in any corner ch-3 sp; ch 3, (2 dc, ch 1, 3 dc) in same sp, ch 1, 3 dc in next ch-3 sp, ch 1, ★ (3 dc, ch 1) twice in next ch-3 sp, 3 dc in next ch-3 sp, ch 1; repeat from ★ around; join with slip st to first dc, finish off: 36 dc.
Rnd 4: With **right** side facing, join CC with sc in any corner ch-1 sp; ch 3, sc in same sp, ch 3, (sc in next ch-1 sp, ch 3) across to next corner ch-1 sp, ★ (sc, ch 3) twice in corner ch-1 sp, (sc in next ch-1 sp, ch 3) across to next corner ch-1 sp; repeat from ★ around; join with slip st to first sc, finish off: 16 ch-3 sps.
Rnd 5: With **right** side facing, join MC with slip st in any corner ch-3 sp; ch 3, (2 dc, ch 1, 3 dc) in same sp, ch 1, (3 dc in next ch-3 sp, ch 1) across to next corner ch-3 sp, ★ (3 dc, ch 1) twice in corner ch-3 sp, (3 dc in next ch-3 sp, ch 1) across to next corner ch-3 sp; repeat from ★ around; join with slip st to first dc, finish off: 60 dc.
Rnds 6-30: Repeat Rnds 4 and 5, 12 times; then repeat Rnd 4 once **more**; at end of Rnd 30, do **not** finish off: 120 ch-3 sps.
Rnds 31 and 32: Slip st in first ch-3 sp, ch 1, (sc, ch 3) twice in same sp, (sc in next ch-3 sp, ch 3) across to next corner ch-3 sp, ★ (sc, ch 3) twice in corner ch-3 sp, (sc in next ch-3 sp, ch 3) across to next corner ch-3 sp; repeat from ★ around; join with slip st to first sc: 128 ch-3 sps.
To work **Picot,** ch 3, slip st in third ch from hook.
Rnd 33: Slip st in first ch-3 sp, ch 3, work (2 dc, Picot, 3 dc, Picot) in same sp, (3 dc in next ch-3 sp, work Picot) across to next corner ch-3 sp, ★ (3 dc, work Picot) twice in corner ch-3 sp, (3 dc in next ch-3 sp, work Picot) across to next corner ch-3 sp; repeat from ★ around; join with slip st to first dc, finish off.

cloud·soft shells

This adorable afghan will wrap your little one in a cloud of softness.
Crocheted using worsted weight brushed acrylic yarn, it features
a pretty shell pattern trimmed with a scalloped edging.

Finished Size: Approximately 35" x 47"

MATERIALS

Worsted Weight Brushed Acrylic Yarn,
   approximately:
      20 ounces, (570 grams, 1,545 yards)
   Crochet hook, size I (5.50 mm) **or** size needed
      for gauge

GAUGE: In pattern,
      (V-St, Shell) twice and 7 rows = 4"

BODY

Ch 124 **loosely**.
To work **V-St**, (dc, ch 1, dc) in st indicated.
To work **Shell**, 5 dc in st indicated.
Row 1: 2 Dc in fourth ch from hook, skip next 3 chs,
work V-St in next ch, ★ skip next 3 chs, work Shell in
next ch, skip next 3 chs, work V-St in next ch; repeat
from ★ across to last 4 chs, skip next 3 chs, 3 dc in
last ch: 14 Shells.
Row 2 (Right side)**:** Ch 3 **(counts as first dc, now
and throughout)**, turn; dc in same st, work Shell in
next V-St (ch-1 sp), ★ work V-St in center dc of next
Shell, work Shell in next V-St; repeat from ★ 13 times
more, 2 dc in last dc.
Note: Loop a short piece of yarn around any stitch to
mark last row as **right** side.
Row 3: Ch 3, turn; 2 dc in same st, work V-St in
center dc of next Shell, ★ work Shell in next V-St,
work V-St in center dc of next Shell; repeat from ★
13 times **more**, 3 dc in last dc.
Repeat Rows 2 and 3 until Afghan measures
approximately 43", ending by working Row 3.
Do **not** finish off.

EDGING

Rnd 1: Ch 1, turn; 3 sc in first dc, sc in each dc
across to last 2 dc, 2 sc in next dc, 3 sc in last dc;
work 150 sc evenly spaced across end of rows;
working in free loops of beginning ch *(Fig. 23b, page
125)*, 3 sc in ch at base of first st, work 103 sc evenly
spaced across to last 2 chs, 2 sc in next ch, 3 sc in last
ch; work 150 sc evenly spaced across end of rows;
join with slip st to first sc: 522 sc.
Rnd 2: Slip st in next sc, ch 4, work V-St in same st,
skip next 2 sc, (work V-St in next sc, skip next 2 sc)
across to next corner sc, ★ dc in corner sc, (ch 1, dc
in same st) twice, skip next 2 sc, (work V-St in next sc,
skip next 2 sc) across to next corner sc; repeat from ★
2 times **more**; join with slip st to third ch of beginning
ch-4.
Rnd 3: Slip st in first ch-1 sp, ch 4, dc in same sp,
work V-St in next dc, ★ work V-St in each ch-1 sp
across to next corner dc, work V-St in corner dc;
repeat from ★ 2 times **more**, work V-St in each ch-1
sp across; join with slip st to third ch of beginning
ch-4.
Rnd 4: Slip st in first ch-1 sp, ch 4, dc in same sp, dc
in next V-St, (ch 1, dc in same st) twice, ★ work V-St
in each V-St across to next corner V-St, dc in corner
V-St, (ch 1, dc in same st) twice; repeat from ★
2 times **more**, work V-St in each V-St across; join
with slip st to third ch of beginning ch-4.
Rnd 5: Slip st in first ch-1 sp, ch 3, 2 dc in same sp,
skip next dc, slip st in next dc, work Shell in next dc,
skip next dc, slip st in next dc, ★ (3 dc in next ch-1 sp,
skip next dc, slip st in next dc) across to next corner
dc, work Shell in corner dc, skip next dc, slip st in next
dc; repeat from ★ 2 times **more**, (3 dc in next ch-1
sp, skip next dc, slip st in next dc) across; join with slip
st to first dc, finish off.

bathed in bubbles

Bathed in bubbles, this lilac-trimmed lovely will lull baby to sleep in no time. Crocheted with baby sport weight yarn, the afghan is made using a combination of pattern stitches, including front and back post double crochets.

Finished Size: Approximately 33" x 33"

MATERIALS
Baby Sport Weight Yarn, approximately:
  MC (White) - 14 ounces,
    (400 grams, 1,415 yards)
  CC (Lilac) - 1 ounce, (30 grams, 100 yards)
Crochet hook, size F (3.75 mm) **or** size needed for gauge

GAUGE: In pattern, 20 sts and 14 rows = 4"

PATTERN STITCHES
FRONT POST DOUBLE CROCHET
(abbreviated FPdc)
YO, insert hook from **front** to **back** around post of st indicated *(Fig. 12, page 123)*, YO and pull up a loop even with last st made, (YO and draw through 2 loops on hook) twice. Skip st behind FPdc.
BACK POST DOUBLE CROCHET
(abbreviated BPdc)
YO, insert hook from **back** to **front** around post of st indicated *(Fig. 13, page 123)*, YO and pull up a loop even with last st made, (YO and draw through 2 loops on hook) twice. Skip st in front of BPdc.

BODY
With MC, ch 151 **loosely**.
Row 1: Sc in second ch from hook and in each ch across: 150 sc.
Note: Dtr should "bubble" to back of work.
Row 2 (Right side): Ch 5 **(counts as first dtr, now and throughout)**, turn; dc in next sc, sc in next sc, (dtr in next sc, dc in next sc, sc in next sc) across.
Note: Loop a short piece of yarn around any stitch to mark last row as **right** side.
Row 3: Ch 5, turn; dc in next dc, sc in next dtr, (dtr in next sc, dc in next dc, sc in next dtr) across.
Repeat Row 3 until Afghan measures approximately 30" from beginning ch, ending by working a **right** side row.
Last Row: Ch 1, turn; sc in each st across; do **not** finish off.

EDGING
Rnd 1: Ch 1, turn; 3 sc in first sc, sc in each sc across to last sc, 3 sc in last sc; work 147 sc evenly spaced across end of rows; working in free loops of beginning ch *(Fig. 23b, page 125)*, 3 sc in first ch, sc in each ch across to last ch, 3 sc in last ch; work 147 sc evenly spaced across end of rows; join with slip st to first sc changing to CC *(Fig. 21b, page 125)*: 602 sc.
Rnd 2: Ch 3 **(counts as first dc, now and throughout)**, turn; dc in next sc and in each sc around working 3 dc in center sc of each corner; join with slip st to first dc: 610 dc.
Rnd 3: Ch 3, turn; work BPdc around next dc, 3 dc in next dc, work (FPdc around next dc, BPdc around next dc) around working 3 dc in center dc of each corner; join with slip st to first dc: 618 sts.
Rnd 4: Ch 3, turn; work BPdc around next st, work (FPdc around next st, BPdc around next st) around working 3 dc in center dc of each corner; join with slip st to first dc: 626 sts.
Rnd 5: Ch 1, turn; sc in each st around working 3 sc in center dc of each corner; join with slip st to first sc, finish off.

dreamy inspiration

Baby will have lots of sweet dreams snuggled in this cozy cover-up crocheted with brushed acrylic yarn! The soft stripes were inspired by nursery ticking fabric.

Finished Size: Approximately 36" x 46"

MATERIALS

Worsted Weight Brushed Acrylic Yarn, approximately:
    MC - 13 ounces, (370 grams, 1,005 yards)
    CC - 9 ounces, (260 grams, 695 yards)
Crochet hook, size I (5.50 mm) **or** size needed for gauge

GAUGE: In pattern, 15 sts and 7 rows = 4"

STRIPE SEQUENCE

2 Rows MC *(Fig. 21a, page 125)*, ★ 1 row CC, 1 row MC, 2 rows CC, 1 row MC, 1 row CC, 4 rows MC; repeat from ★ for sequence, ending by working 2 rows MC.

BODY

With MC, ch 133 **loosely**.
To work **V-St**, (dc, ch 1, dc) in st or sp indicated.
Row 1 (Right side)**:** Work V-St in fifth ch from hook **(first 3 skipped chs count as first dc)**, ★ skip next 2 chs, 3 dc in next ch, skip next 2 chs, work V-St in next ch; repeat from ★ across to last 2 chs, skip next ch, dc in last ch: 21 3-dc groups.
Rows 2-80: Ch 3 **(counts as first dc, now and throughout)**, turn; skip next dc, work V-St in next ch-1 sp, ★ skip next 2 dc, 3 dc in next dc, skip next 2 dc, work V-St in next ch-1 sp; repeat from ★ across to last 2 dc, skip next dc, dc in last dc.
Do **not** finish off.

EDGING

Rnd 1: With CC ch 1, turn; 3 sc in first dc, sc in each dc across to last dc, 3 sc in last dc; work 151 sc evenly spaced across end of rows; working in free loops of beginning ch *(Fig. 23b, page 125)*, 3 sc in first ch, work 107 sc evenly spaced across to next corner ch, 3 sc in corner ch; work 151 sc evenly spaced across end of rows; join with slip st to first sc: 528 sc.
Rnd 2: Ch 1, (sc, ch 3, slip st) in same st, slip st in next sc, ★ (sc, ch 3, slip st) in next sc, slip st in next sc; repeat from ★ around; join with slip st to first sc, finish off.

general instructions

BASIC INFORMATION

YARN

Yarn listed under Materials for each afghan in this book is given in a generic weight. Once you know the weight of the yarn, any brand of the same weight may be used. This enables you to purchase the brand of yarn you like best.

You may wish to purchase a single skein first and crochet a gauge swatch. Compare the way your swatch looks to the photograph to be sure that you will be satisfied with the results. How many skeins to buy depends on the yardage. Ounces and grams will vary from one brand of the same weight to another, but the yardage required will always remain the same, provided gauge is met and maintained.

GAUGE

Gauge is the number of stitches and rows or rounds per inch and is used to determine the finished size. All crochet patterns will specify the gauge that you must match to ensure proper size and to be sure you have enough yarn to complete the project. Hook sizes given in instructions are merely guides. Because everyone crochets differently - loosely, tightly, or somewhere in between - the finished size can vary, even when crocheters use the very same pattern, yarn, and hook. Before beginning any crocheted item, it is absolutely necessary for you to crochet a gauge swatch in the pattern stitch indicated with the weight of yarn and hook size suggested. Your swatch must be large enough to measure your gauge. Lay your swatch on a hard, smooth, flat surface. Then measure it, counting your stitches and rows or rounds carefully. If your swatch is smaller than specified or you have too many stitches per inch, try again with a larger size hook; if your swatch is larger or you don't have enough stitches per inch, try again with a smaller size hook. Keep trying until you find the size that will give you the specified gauge. DO NOT HESITATE TO CHANGE HOOK SIZE TO OBTAIN CORRECT GAUGE. Once proper gauge is obtained, measure width of piece approximately every 3" to be sure gauge remains consistent.

ABBREVIATIONS

BPdc	Back Post double crochet(s)
CC	Contrasting Color
ch(s)	chain(s)
dc	double crochet(s)
dtr	double treble crochet(s)
ex Ldc	extended Long double crochet
FPdc	Front Post double crochet(s)
hdc	half double crochet(s)
Ldc	Long double crochet(s)
MC	Main Color
mm	millimeters
Rnd(s)	Round(s)
sc	single crochet(s)
sp(s)	space(s)
st(s)	stitch(es)
tr	treble crochet(s)
YO	yarn over

★ — work instructions following ★ as many **more** times as indicated in addition to the first time.

† to † — work all instructions from first † to second † **as many** times as specified.

( ) or [ ] — work enclosed instructions **as many** times as specified by the number immediately following **or** work all enclosed instructions in the stitch or space indicated **or** contains explanatory remarks.

BASIC STITCH GUIDE

CHAIN

When beginning a first row of crochet in a chain, always skip the first ch from the hook and work into the second ch from the hook (for single crochet), third chain from the hook (for half double crochet), or fourth chain from the hook (for double crochet), etc. *(Fig. 1)*.

Fig. 1

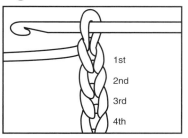

WORKING INTO THE CHAIN

Method 1: Insert hook into back ridge of each chain *(Fig. 2a)*.
Method 2: Insert hook under top two strands of each chain *(Fig. 2b)*.

Fig. 2a   **Fig. 2b**

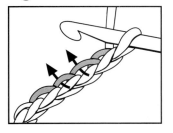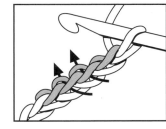

SLIP STITCH *(abbreviated slip st)*

This stitch is used to attach new yarn, to join work, or to move the yarn across a group of stitches without adding height. Insert hook in stitch or space indicated, YO and draw through stitch **and** through loop on hook *(Fig. 3)*.

Fig. 3

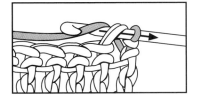

MAKING A BEGINNING RING

Chain amount indicated in instructions. Being careful not to twist chain, slip stitch in first chain to form a ring *(Fig. 4)*.

Fig. 4

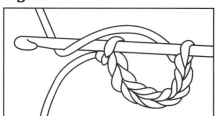

SINGLE CROCHET *(abbreviated sc)*

Insert hook in stitch or space indicated, YO and pull up a loop, YO and draw through both loops on hook *(Fig. 5)*.

Fig. 5

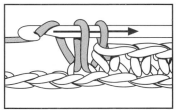

HALF DOUBLE CROCHET *(abbreviated hdc)*

YO, insert hook in stitch or space indicated, YO and pull up a loop (3 loops on hook), YO and draw through all 3 loops on hook *(Fig. 6)*.

Fig. 6

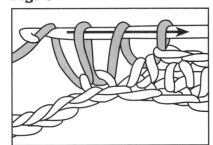

DOUBLE CROCHET
(abbreviated dc)

YO, insert hook in stitch or space indicated, YO and pull up a loop (3 loops on hook), YO and draw through 2 loops on hook *(Fig. 7a)*, YO and draw through remaining 2 loops on hook *(Fig. 7b)*.

Fig. 7a

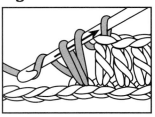

Fig. 7b

LONG DOUBLE CROCHET
(abbreviated Ldc)

YO, insert hook in stitch or space indicated, YO and pull up a loop even with loop on hook (3 loops on hook) *(Fig. 8)*, (YO and draw through 2 loops on hook) twice.

Fig. 8

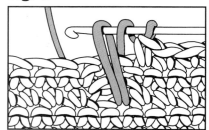

TREBLE CROCHET *(abbreviated tr)*

YO twice, insert hook in stitch or space indicated, YO and pull up a loop (4 loops on hook) *(Fig. 9a)*, (YO and draw through 2 loops on hook) 3 times *(Fig. 9b)*.

Fig. 9a

Fig. 9b

DOUBLE TREBLE CROCHET
(abbreviated dtr)

YO 3 times, insert hook in stitch or space indicated, YO and pull up a loop (5 loops on hook) *(Fig. 10a)*, (YO and draw through 2 loops on hook) 4 times *(Fig. 10b)*.

Fig. 10a

Fig. 10b

PATTERN STITCHES

POST STITCH

Work around post of stitch indicated, inserting hook in direction of arrow *(Fig. 11)*.

Fig. 11

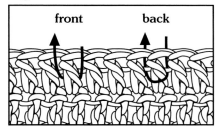

FRONT POST DOUBLE CROCHET *(abbreviated FPdc)*

YO, insert hook from **front** to **back** around post of stitch indicated, YO and pull up a loop (3 loops on hook) *(Fig. 12)*, (YO and draw through 2 loops on hook) twice.

Fig. 12

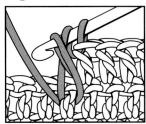

BACK POST DOUBLE CROCHET *(abbreviated BPdc)*

YO, insert hook from **back** to **front** around post of stitch indicated, YO and pull up a loop (3 loops on hook) *(Fig. 13)*, (YO and draw through 2 loops on hook) twice.

Fig. 13

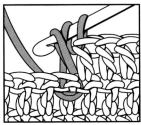

CLUSTER

A Cluster can be worked all in the same stitch or space *(Figs. 14a & b)*, **or** across several stitches *(Figs. 15a & b)*.

Fig. 14a

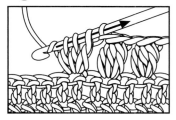

Fig. 14b

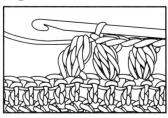

Fig. 15a

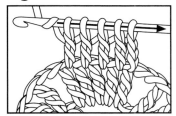

Fig. 15b

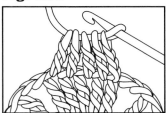

POPCORN

Work number of dc specified in stitch or space indicated, drop loop from hook, insert hook in first dc of dc group, hook dropped loop and draw through *(Figs. 16a & b)*.

Fig. 16a (4-dc Popcorn)

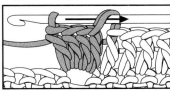

Fig. 16b (5-dc Popcorn)

PUFF STITCH

Work as instructed for each design *(Fig. 17)*.

Fig. 17

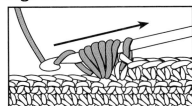

REVERSE SINGLE CROCHET
(abbreviated reverse sc)
Working from **left** to **right**, insert hook in stitch or space to right of hook *(Fig. 18a)*, YO and draw through, under and to left of loop on hook (2 loops on hook) *(Fig. 18b)*, YO and draw through both loops on hook *(Figs. 18c & d)*.

Fig. 18a

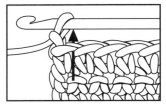

Fig. 18b

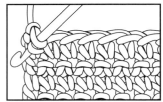

Fig. 18c

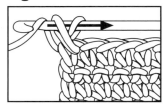

Fig. 18d

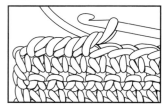

REVERSE HALF DOUBLE CROCHET *(abbreviated reverse hdc)*
Working from **left** to **right**, YO, insert hook in stitch or space to right of hook *(Fig. 19a)*, YO and draw through, under and to left of loops on hook (3 loops on hook) *(Fig. 19b)*, YO and draw through all 3 loops on hook *(Figs. 19c & d)*.

Fig. 19a

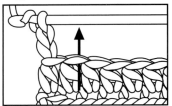

Fig. 19b

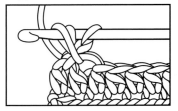

Fig. 19c

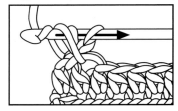

Fig. 19d

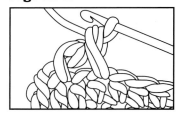

STITCHING TIPS

HOW TO DETERMINE THE RIGHT SIDE

Many designs are made with the **front** of the stitch as the **right** side. Notice that the **fronts** of the stitches are smooth *(Fig. 20a)* and the **backs** of the stitches are bumpy *(Fig. 20b)*. For easy identification, it may be helpful to loop a short piece of yarn around any stitch to mark **right** side.

Fig. 20a

Fig. 20b

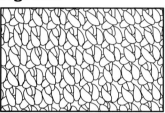

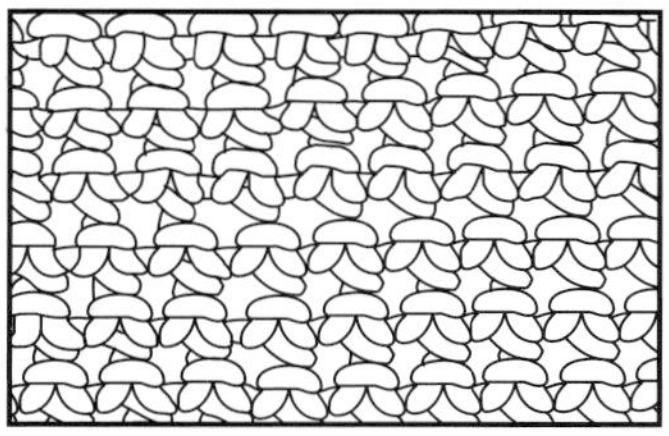

JOINING WITH SC

When instructed to join with sc, begin with a slip knot on hook. Insert hook in stitch or space indicated, YO and pull up a loop, YO and draw through both loops on hook.

CHANGING COLORS

Work the last stitch to within one step of completion, hook new yarn *(Fig. 21a)* and draw through all loops on hook. Cut old yarn and work over both ends unless otherwise specified. When working in rounds, drop old yarn and join with slip st to first stitch using new yarn *(Fig. 21b)*.

Fig. 21a

Fig. 21b

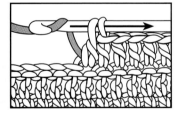

BACK OR FRONT LOOP ONLY

Work only in loop(s) indicated by arrow *(Fig. 22)*.

Fig. 22

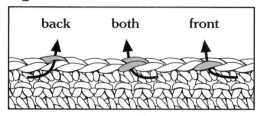

back   both   front

FREE LOOPS

After working in Back or Front Loops Only on a row or round, there will be a ridge of unused loops. These are called the free loops. Later, when instructed to work into the free loops of the same row or round, work in these loops *(Fig. 23a)*.

When instructed to work in free loops of a beginning chain, work in loop indicated by arrow *(Fig. 23b)*.

Fig. 23a

Fig. 23b

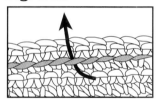

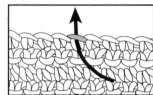

NO-SEW JOINING

Hold Squares, Motifs, or Strips with **wrong** sides together. Work slip stitch or sc into space as indicated *(Fig. 24)*.

Fig. 24

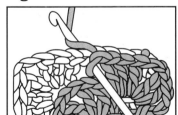

125

FINISHING

SEAMS

A tapestry or yarn needle is best to use for sewing seams because the blunt point will not split the yarn as easily as a sewing needle. Use the same yarn the item was made with to sew the seams. However, if the yarn is textured or bulky, it may be easier to sew the seam with a small, smooth yarn of the same color, such as tapestry yarn or an acrylic needlepoint yarn. If a different yarn is used for the seams, be sure the care instructions for both yarns are the same. If the yarn used to crochet the item is machine washable, the seam yarn must also be machine washable.

WHIPSTITCH

With **wrong** sides together and beginning in corner stitch, sew through both pieces once to secure the beginning of the seam, leaving an ample yarn end to weave in later. Insert the needle from **front** to **back** through **both** loops of **each** piece *(Fig. 25a)* **or** through **inside** loops only *(Fig. 25b)*. Bring the needle around and insert it from **front** to **back** through the next loops of **both** pieces. Continue in this manner across to corner, keeping the sewing yarn fairly loose and being careful to match stitches.

Fig. 25a

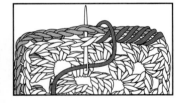

Fig. 25b

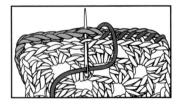

BLOCKING

Blocking "sets" a crocheted item and smooths the stitches to give your work a professional appearance. Before blocking, check the yarn label for any special instructions, because many acrylics and some blends may be damaged during blocking.

Note: Always use stainless steel pins.

Steaming is an excellent method of blocking crocheted afghans, especially those made with **wool or wool blends**. Turn the afghan wrong side up and pin it to the correct size on a board covered with towels. Hold a steam iron or steamer just above the afghan and steam it thoroughly. Never let the weight of the iron touch the afghan because it will flatten the stitches. Leave the afghan pinned until it is completely dry. On fragile **acrylics** that can be blocked, pin the item to the correct size on a towel-covered board, and cover the item with dampened bath towels. When the towels are dry, the item is blocked.

FRINGE

Cut a piece of cardboard 3" wide and ½" longer than you want your finished fringe to be. Wind the yarn **loosely** and **evenly** lengthwise around the cardboard until the card is filled, then cut across one end; repeat as needed.

Align half as many strands of yarn as desired for the finished fringe and fold in half.

With **wrong** side facing and using a crochet hook, draw the folded end up through a stitch or rows and pull the loose ends through the folded end *(Figs. 26a & c)*; draw the knot up **tightly** *(Figs. 26b & d)*. Repeat, spacing as desired.

Lay flat on a hard surface and trim the ends.

Fig. 26a

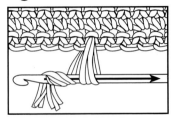

Fig. 26b

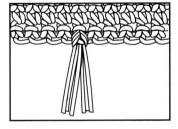

Fig. 26c

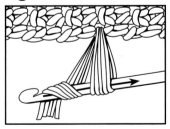

Fig. 26d

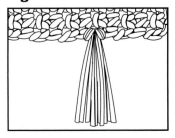